ANDREAS GEFELLER

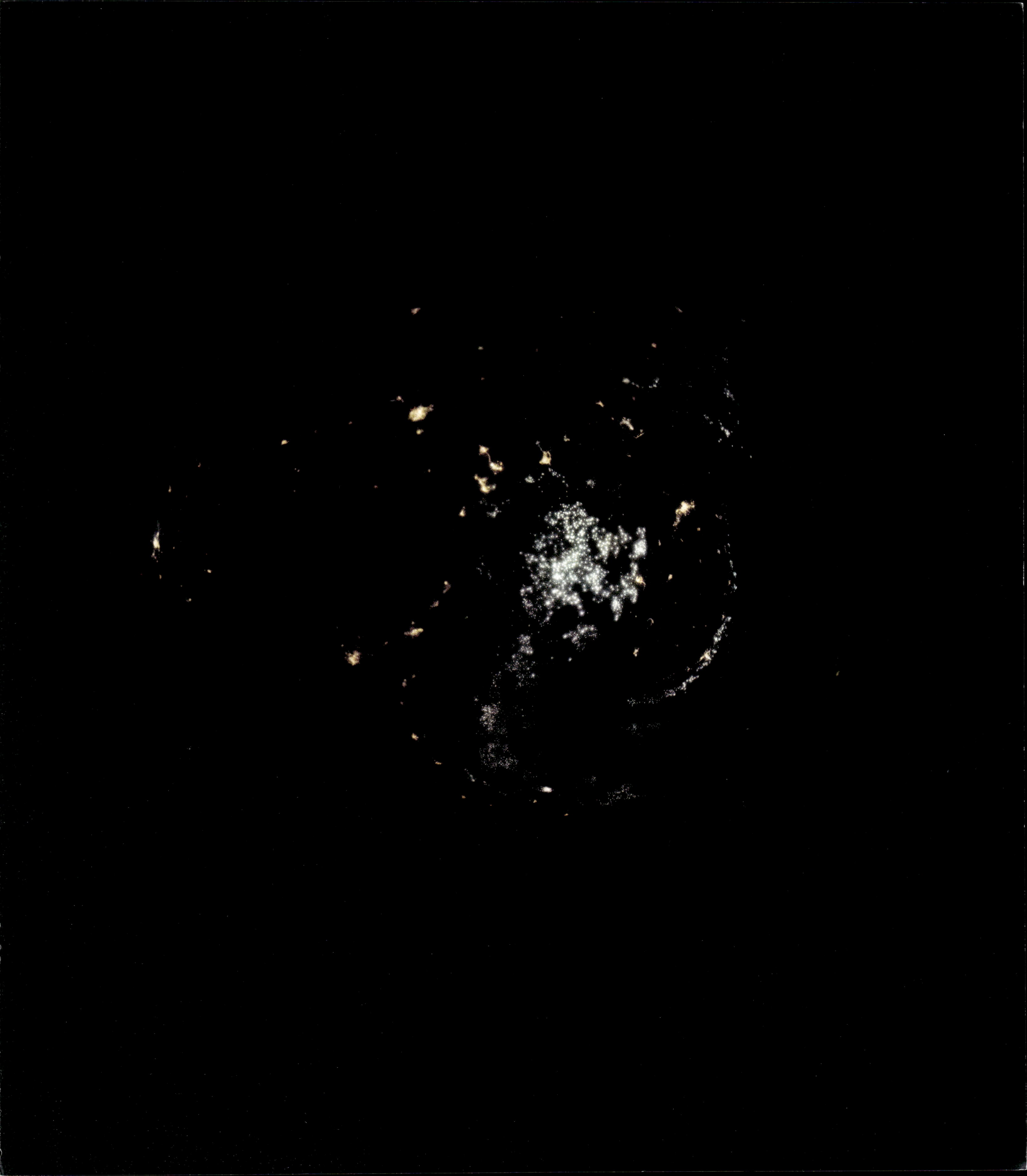

ANDREAS GEFELLER

BLANK

WITH AN ESSAY BY MIT EINEM ESSAY VON

DAVID CAMPANY

HATJE
CANTZ

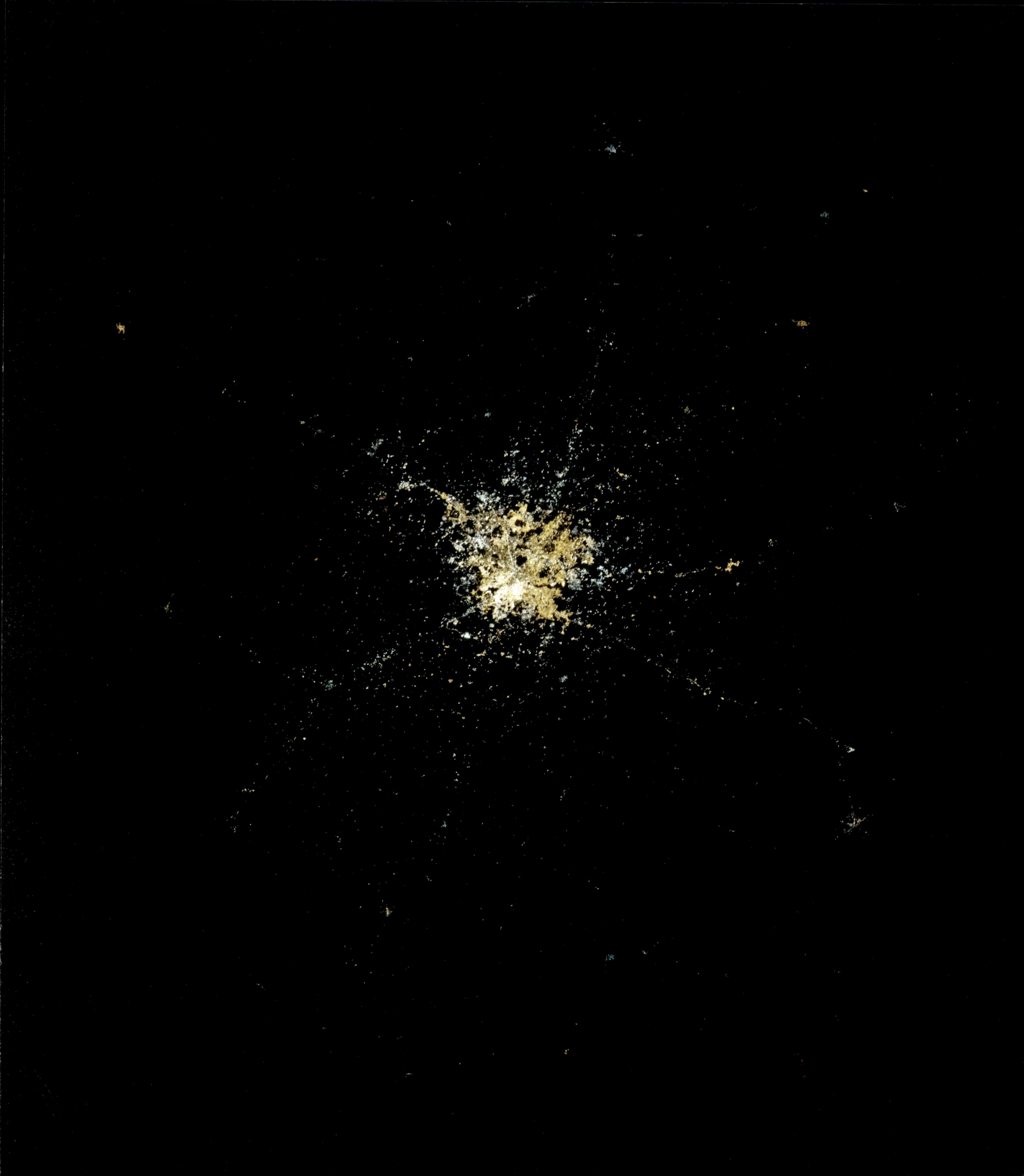

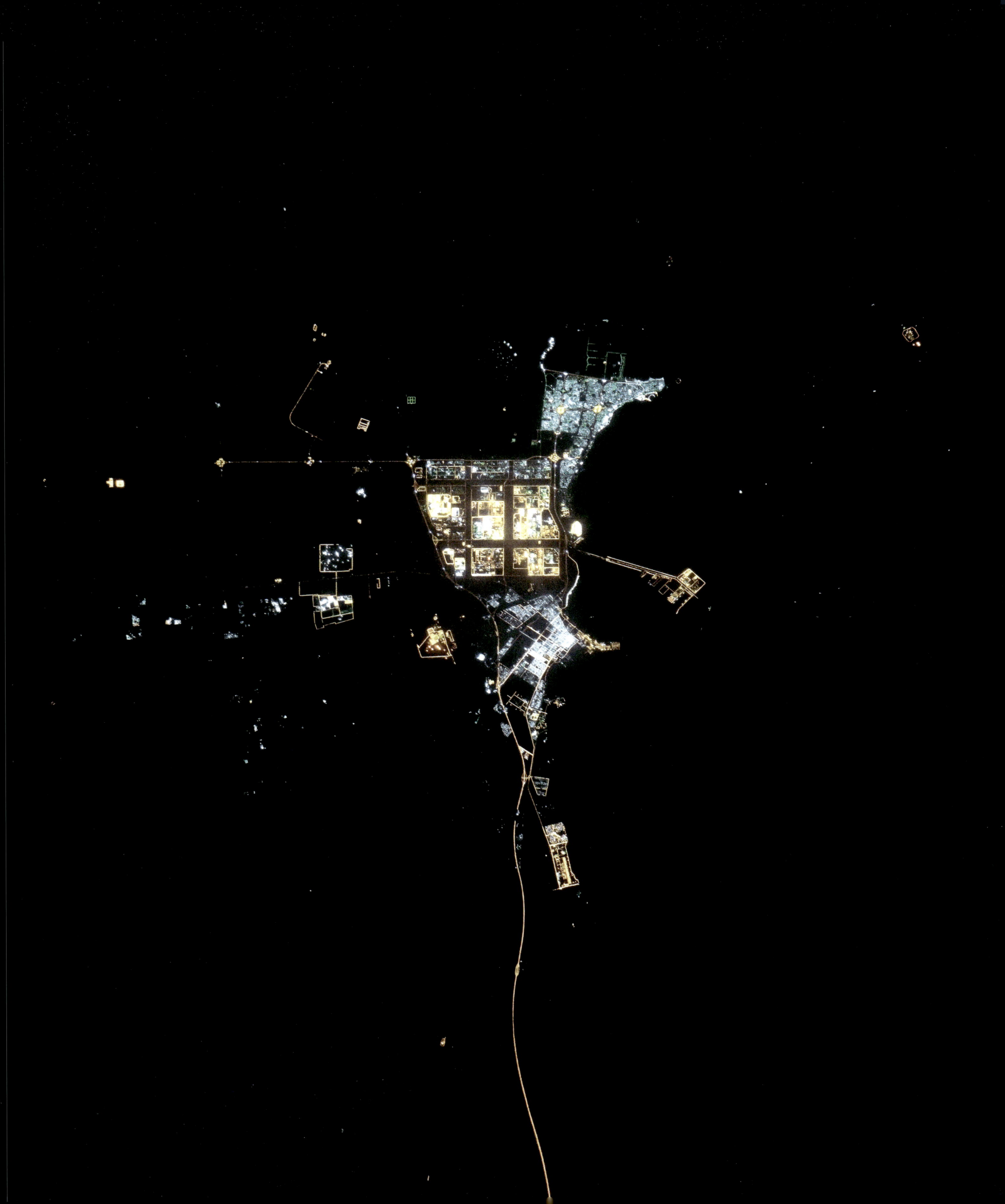

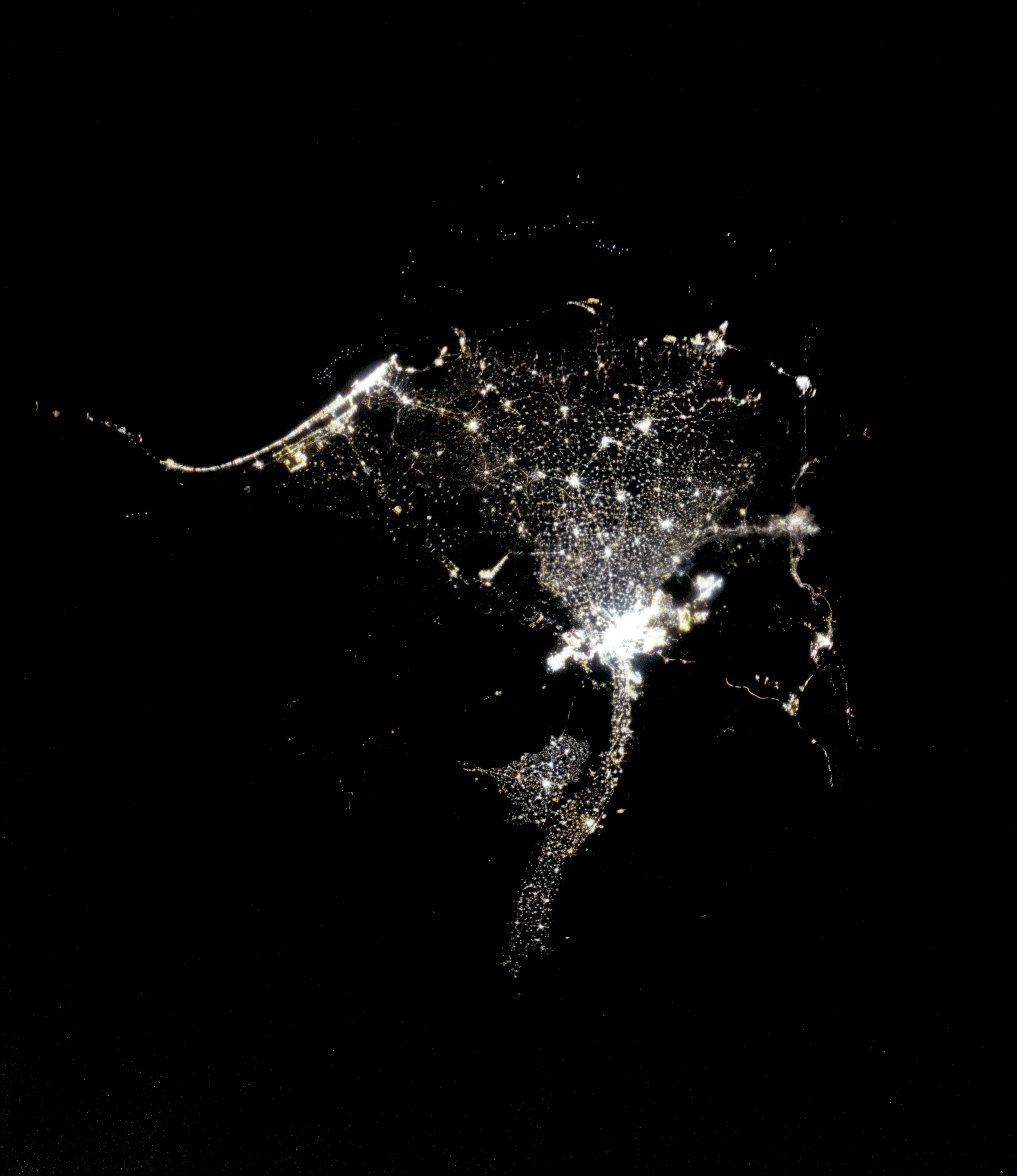

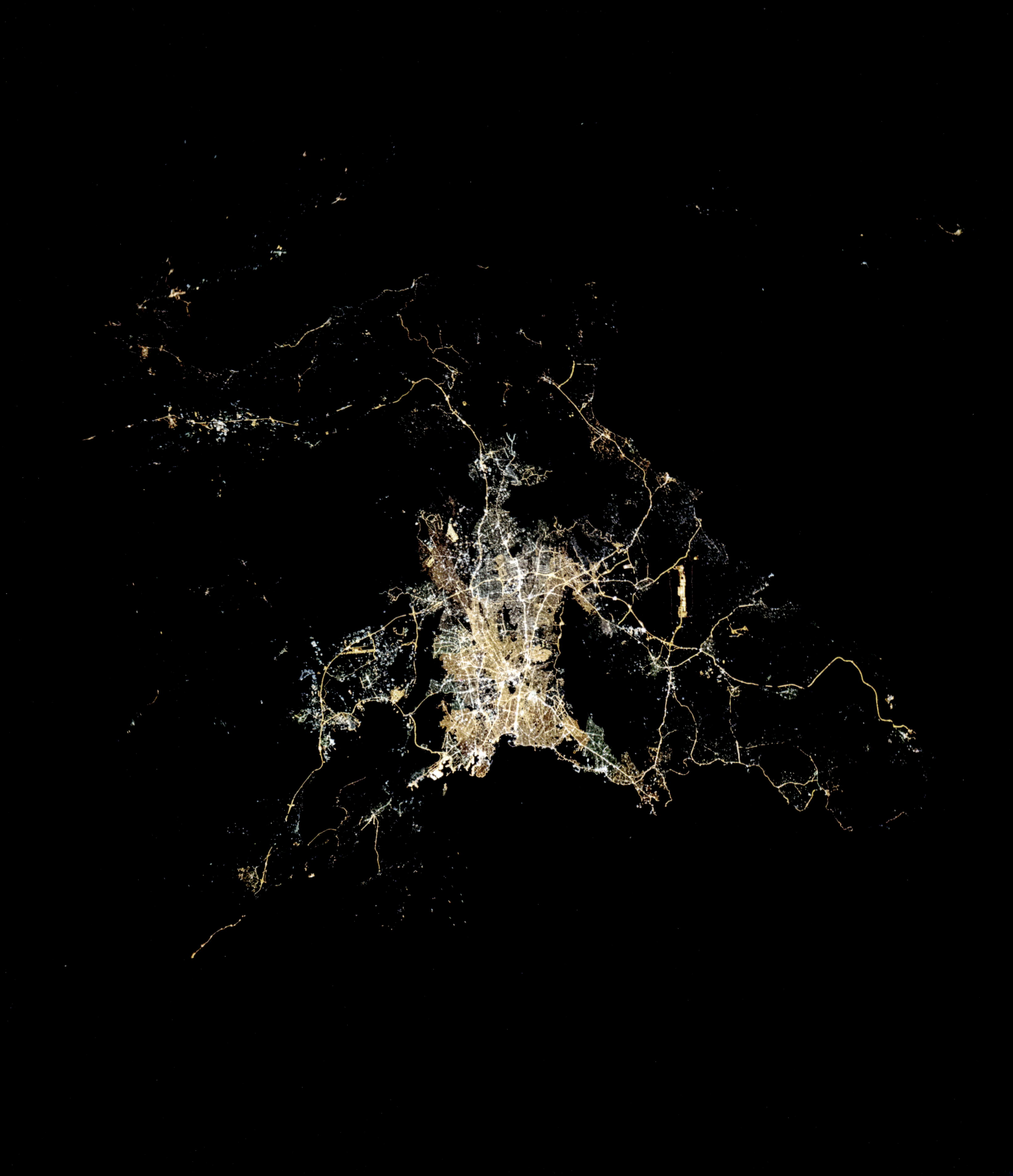

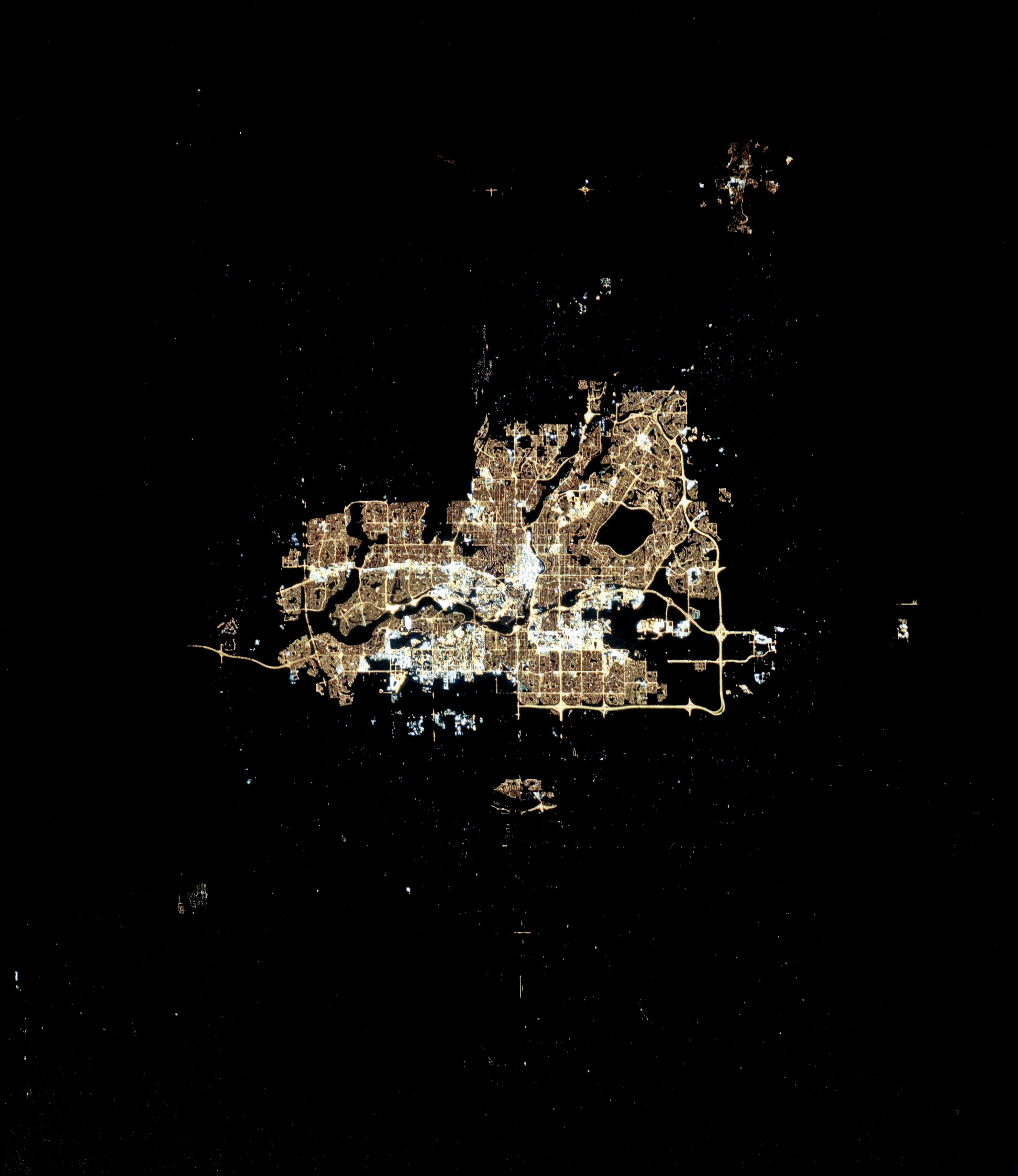

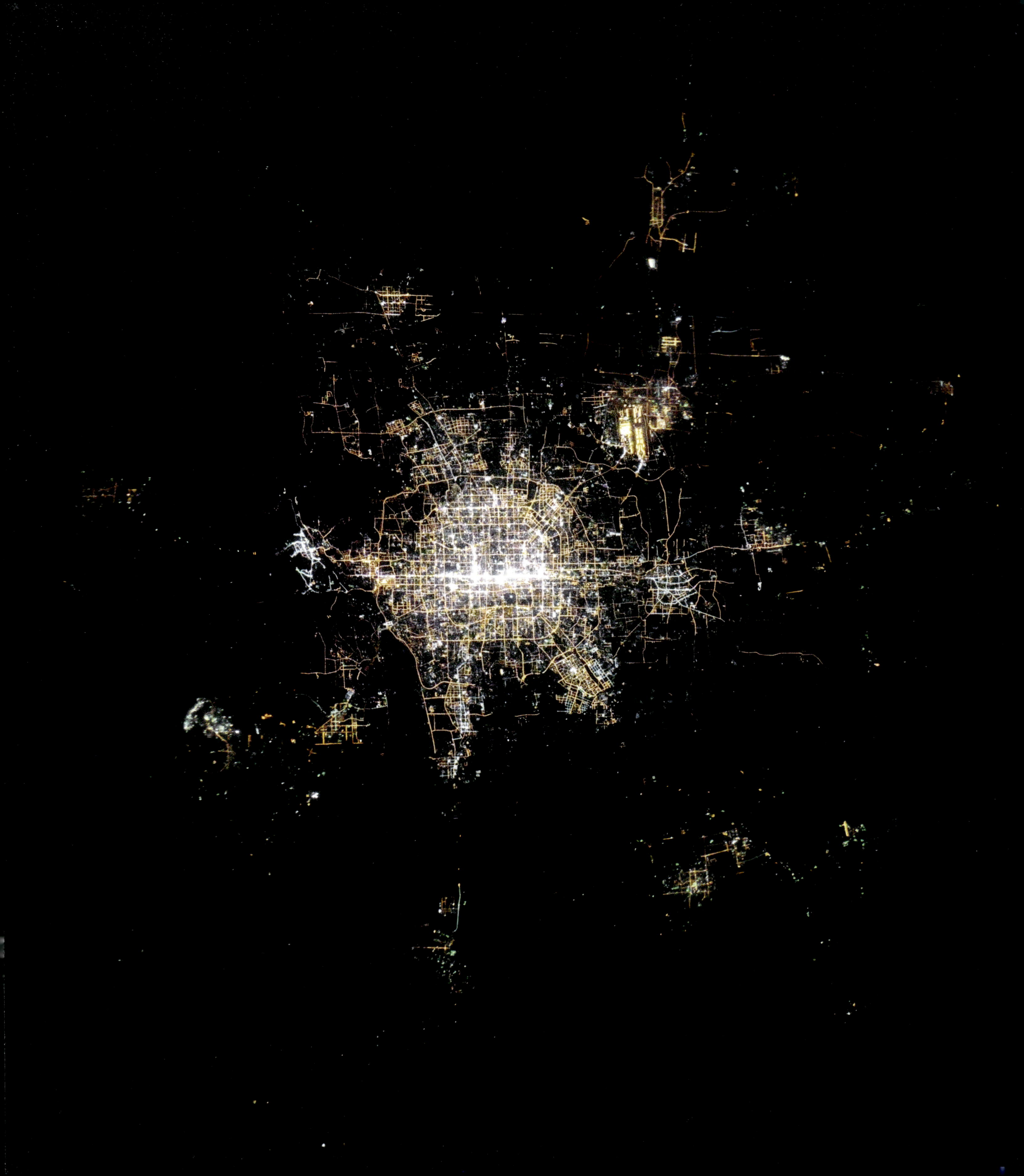

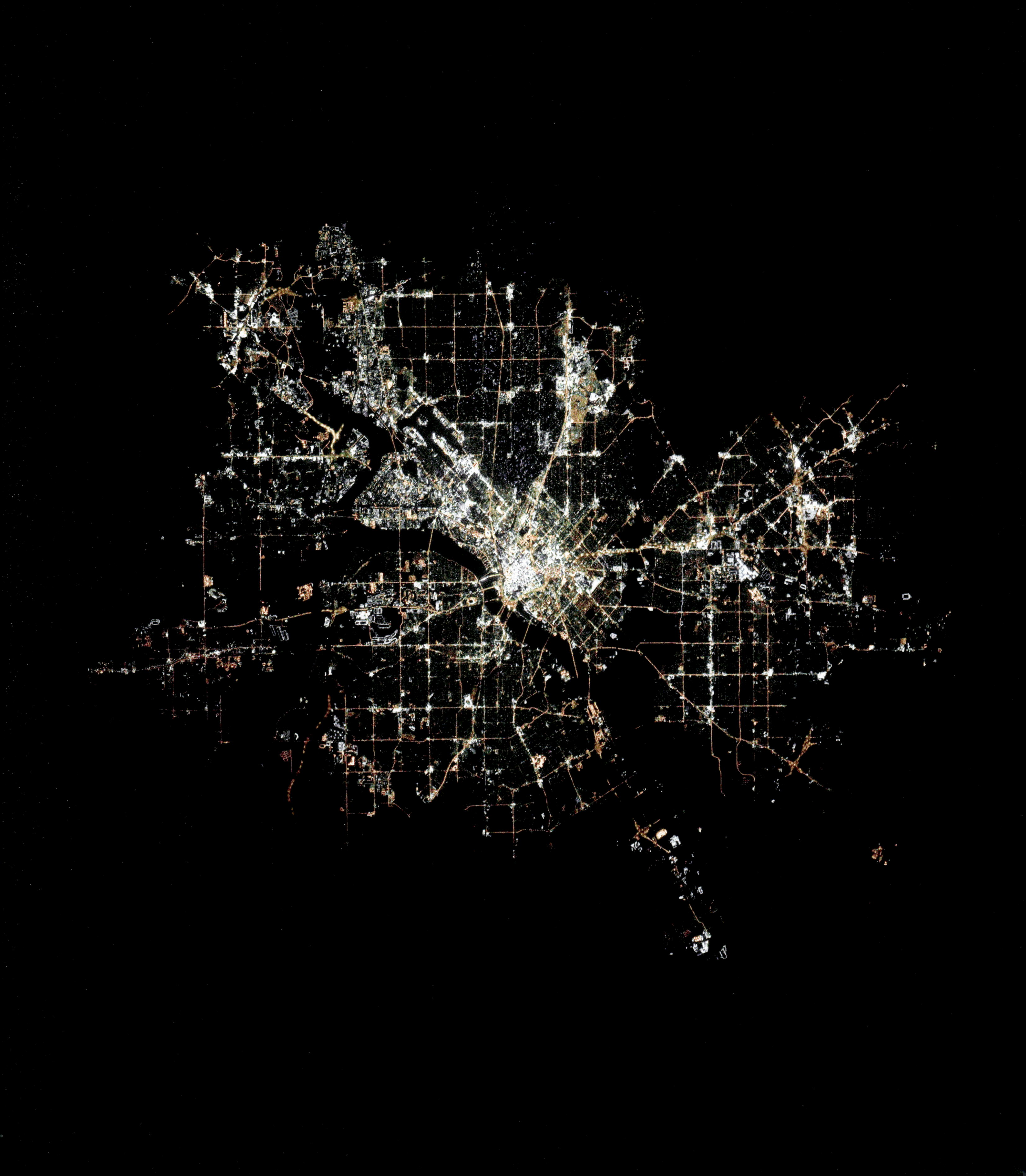

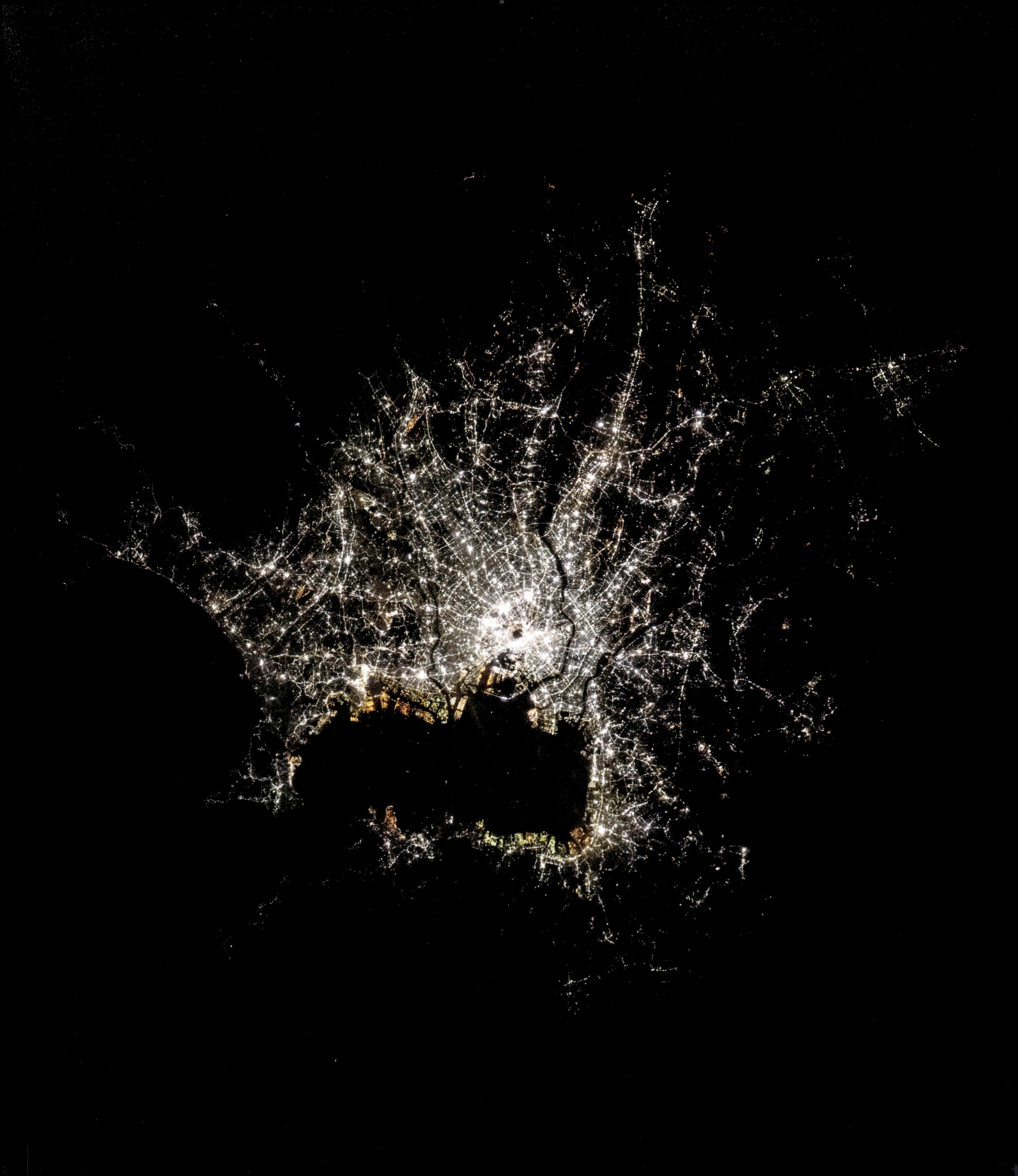

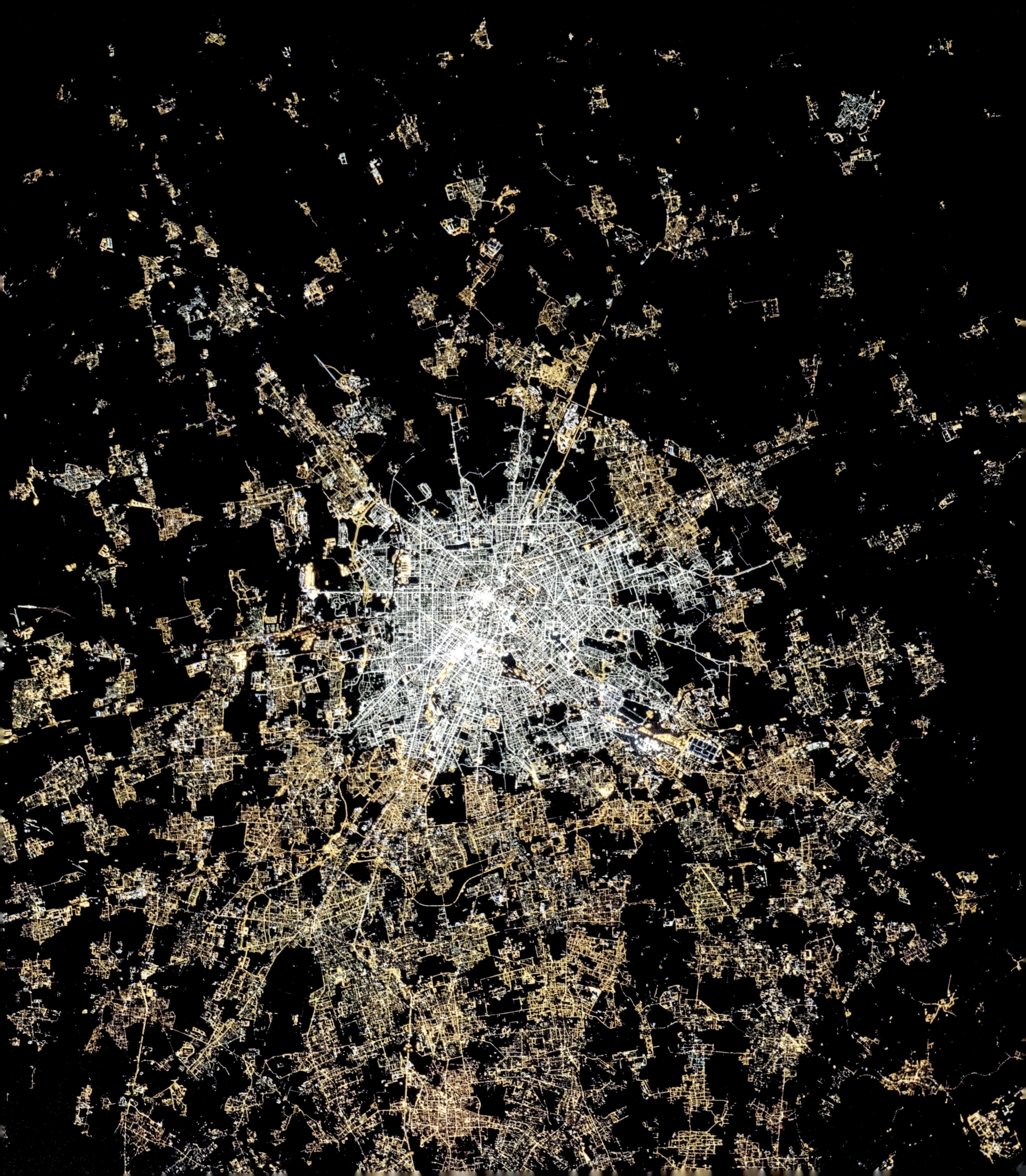

DOOMED TO SEE
ZUM SEHEN VERURTEILT

DAVID CAMPANY

Our metaphors of light are ubiquitous and profound, and have lasted for millennia. Everyday language is full of them, and they are used so often without even a second thought. We talk of knowledge as *illumination*. We are *exposed* to new ideas, and *overexposed* to too many. When we are confused, we are *in the dark*. Ignorance is a form of *blindness*. Hope is the *light at the end of the tunnel*. Intelligen people are *bright*; the unintelligent are *dim*. When a cartoon character gets an idea, a shining ligh bulb appears above their head. New ideas come *in a flash*. The turn from superstition to reason was a turn to *enlightenment*. Meanwhile the superstitious texts of religion contain endless references to *shining paths*, to *God as light*, *light as wisdom*, and *light as truth*. The unbelieving are *banished into darkness*. And if you understand, you *see what I mean*.

When a baby is born it receives more stimulus through the eyes than any other part of the body, except the mouth. The photographer Walker Evans often referred to his “hungry eye,” as if the stimulation gained by seeing was akin to the sustenance gained by swallowing. “Stare,” he implored. “It is the way to educate your eye, and more. Stare, pry listen, eavesdrop. Die knowing something. You are not here long.”[1] The camera has a mouth too, and it swallows the world. But it swallows without chewing, because it cannot do that. We then ask the camera to spit out what it has swallowed onto a screen or onto paper. We must then re-swallow it with our own eyes.

We are told we live in an age of enormous *visual appetites*. We run the risk of an *obesity of vision*, of swallowing more appearances than is good for us. We are told this by the very media outlets that are producing this glut of visibility. It is a misdiagnosis, based on the idea that it is the amount of images in the world that is the source of the problem. In fact the problem

Unsere Metaphern für Licht sind allgegenwärtig und tief greifend und sie sind seit Jahrtausenden gültig. Jede Sprache ist voll von ihnen und oftmals werden sie angewendet, ohne dass auch nur ein zweiter Gedanke an sie verschwendet würde. Wir sprechen vom Wissen als *Erleuchtung.* Sind wir verwirrt, *tappen wir im Dunkeln.* Ignoranz ist eine Form von *Blindheit.* Hoffnung ist *das Licht am Ende des Tunnels.* Intelligente Menschen sind *helle Köpfchen,* die weniger intelligenten indes *keine Leuchten* oder gar *unterbelichtet.* Hat die Figur in einem Cartoon eine plötzliche Eingebung, erscheint eine leuchtende Glühbirne über ihrem Kopf. Neue Ideen kommen einem *blitzartig.* Der Übergang vom Aberglauben zur Vernunft wird als *Erleuchtung* bezeichnet. Währenddessen enthalten die auf dem Aberglauben basierenden religiösen Texte unzählige Bezüge zu *leuchtenden Pfaden, Gott als Licht, Licht als Weisheit* und *Licht als Wahrheit.* Die Ungläubigen werden hingegen *in die Finsternis verbannt.* Und versteht man etwas, dann *sieht* man, was der andere meint.

Ein Neugeborenes empfängt über die Augen mehr Reize als über jeden anderen Körperteil, mit Ausnahme des Mundes. Der Fotograf Walker Evans bezog sich oftmals auf sein »hungriges Auge«, ganz so, als ähnele der durch das Sehen erzeugte Reiz jener Versorgung mit Nahrung, die durch das Schlucken erfolgt. So bat er inständig: »Anstarren. Es ist der Weg, sein Auge zu erziehen, und noch mehr. Anstarren, spionieren, horchen, lauschen. Stirb mit etwas, das du weißt. Du bist hier nicht allzu lange.«[1] Auch die Kamera verfügt über einen Mund, und sie schluckt damit die Welt. Doch sie schluckt, ohne zu kauen, da sie dies nicht vermag. Wir verlangen dann von der Kamera, dass sie das, was sie geschluckt hat, auf einen Bildschirm oder auf Papier ausspuckt. Letztlich müssen wir es mit unseren eigenen Augen nochmals schlucken.

(if it *is* a problem) stems from the image itself. It is in the nature of images, *all* images, *any* image, to offer us more than we want and not enough of what we want. Images can leave us bloated but still hungry. Images exceed meaning in ways that are unruly, even treacherous. At the same time they are inevitably elusive and enigmatic. René Magritte called it the "treason of images." This is why the image world is so bound up by the conventions of genre and the law of language (caption, title, commentary). But in the last instance images remain anarchic, and this is why they have always been a source of great attraction and great suspicion. Yes, we may well live in a hyper-optical culture, in which the eye is stimulated as never before. But visual stimulation is neither knowledge nor understanding, although it can play a part in both.

The anxiety that the world of images might disturb or distort civil society is familiar. How often do we hear that we are "bombarded" or "under siege" from pictures, as if somehow they were pursuing us? How often are we told we are *overexposed*? And in that narcissism we may delude ourselves that it is a new problem, afflicting only us, and only now. The arrival of photography in the eighteen-thirties and its subsequent development into a mass medium certainly introduced new problems, new pleasures, and new disturbances into the family of images. But these have only exacerbated the essentially unpredictable condition of the image as such.

Instead, the real challenge we face has to do with the relation between appearance and meaning, or appearance and revelation. Photography was a product of the Industrial Revolution, and so it had a kinship with those industrial technologies that were discernible to the human eye, that could be understood visually. This was the world of pulleys and levers, of mechanical clocks and Aristotelian principles. One could look at a photograph of a steam engine and figure out how it worked. The relation between the mechanical world and photography was complementary. An optical-mechanical-chemical camera for a legible-mechanical-chemical world. Of course photography could not reveal the economics of mechanized industrialism, at least not in any immediate way. This is why Walter Benjamin was so suspicious of photography's promise of revelation. "A photograph of the Krupp works or the AEG tells us nothing about these institutions. Actual reality has slipped into the functional. The reification of human relations—the factory, say—means that they are no longer explicit," he wrote back in 1931.[2] But really those relations were never truly explicit, never fully revealed to vision alone. A photograph might be able to show how a machine works but it cannot tell you who owns it, or how much its operator is paid, or how much profit is generated.

At a later point, let's say in the years following the Second World War, that world of machines was complicated even further by the rapid spread of the electronic world of the computer and its *invisible* activities. This is our era of

Uns wird erzählt, dass wir in einem Zeitalter enormen *visuellen Appetits* leben. Wir laufen Gefahr, eine *Fettleibigkeit des Blickes* zu erleiden, mehr an äußerem Schein zu schlucken, als uns guttut. Das erzählen uns genau jene Medienkanäle, die diese Flut an Sichtbarkeit hervorbringen. Es handelt sich dabei um eine Fehldiagnose, basierend auf der Vorstellung, dass es die Menge an Bildern auf der Welt ist, die die Quelle der Probleme darstellt. Tatsächlich entspringt das Problem (wenn es denn ein Problem *ist)* dem Bild selbst. Es liegt in der Natur des Bildes, *aller* Bilder, *jeglicher* Bilder, uns mehr zu zeigen, als wir wollen, und nicht genug von dem, was wir wollen. Bilder können uns aufgebläht, jedoch immer noch hungrig zurücklassen. Bilder übersteigen die Bedeutung auf eine Weise, die widerspenstig, geradezu heimtückisch ist. Zugleich sind sie zwangsläufig trügerisch und rätselhaft. René Magritte bezeichnete das als »Verrat der Bilder«. Aus diesem Grund ist die Welt der Bilder so sehr den Konventionen des Genres und dem Gesetz der Sprache (Bildunterschrift, Titel, Kommentar) verhaftet. In letzter Instanz aber bleiben Bilder gesetzlos und genau deshalb sind sie seit jeher die Quelle großer Anziehungskraft und großen Misstrauens. Ja, wir mögen zwar in einer hyper-optischen Kultur leben, in der das Auge so vielen Reizen wie niemals zuvor ausgesetzt ist, doch visuelle Stimulation ist weder gleichzusetzen mit Wissen noch mit Verstehen, obwohl sie für beides eine Rolle spielen kann.

Die Angst, dass die Welt der Bilder die bürgerliche Gesellschaft stören oder gar verfälschen könnte, ist vertraut. Wie oft hören wir, dass Bilder uns »bombardieren« oder »überschwemmen«, als ob sie uns irgendwie verfolgen würden. Wie oft erzählt man uns, wir seien zu exponiert? Und in diesem Narzissmus machen wir uns bisweilen selbst vor, dass es sich dabei um ein neues Problem handele, das nur uns betreffe und nur heutzutage auftrete. Das Aufkommen der Fotografie in den 1830er-Jahren und ihre anschließende Entwicklung zum Massenmedium führten zweifellos zu neuen Problemen, neuen Freuden und neuen Unruhen in der Familie der Bilder. Diese Probleme haben jedoch den grundsätzlich unberechenbaren Charakter des Bildes per se lediglich verstärkt.

Stattdessen liegt die wahre Herausforderung, vor die wir uns gestellt sehen, in der Beziehung zwischen Erscheinung und Bedeutung oder Erscheinung und Enthüllung. Die Fotografie war ein Produkt der industriellen Revolution und somit verwandt mit jenen industriellen Technologien, die für das menschliche Auge wahrnehmbar waren, die also visuell begriffen werden konnten. Das war die Welt der Flaschenzüge und Hebel, der mechanischen Uhren und aristotelischen Prinzipien. Man konnte die Fotografie einer Dampfmaschine betrachten und sich zusammenreimen, wie diese funktionierte. Die Beziehung zwischen mechanischer Welt und Fotografie war komplementär. Eine optisch-mechanisch-chemische Kamera für eine lesbare mechanisch-chemische Welt. Natürlich war die Fotografie nicht in der Lage, die Ökonomie des mechanisierten Industrialismus zu enthüllen

we want from our eyes and what it is we want from what they see. What is vision for when the real forces that affect our lives have become invisible? Does the image world offer insight or distraction? Is vision being eclipsed? Would we be better off not looking?

When a baby is born it receives more stimulus through the eyes than any other part of the body except the mouth. The photographer Walker Evans often referred to his "hungry eye."

Yes, we may well live in a visual culture,

At a later point let's say in the years following the second world war, that world of images was complicated even further by the age of electronic

looking? Should we give up on vision? Could we give up on it?

What is vision for when the real forces that affect our lives have become invisible? Does the image world offer insight or distraction? Is vision being eclipsed? Would we be better off not looking? And yet we still have eyes

… Fotografien in unserem Laptop, so bleibt dem Glasauge der Kamera nichts anderes übrig, als verständnislos auf die eigene Unzulänglichkeit zu starren. Paradoxerweise hat diese Computerisierung, mit ihren ausgedehnten Netzwerken und einfachen Wiedergaben, ihre eigene Ausweitung und …

… dessen schaffen, was wir von unseren Augen verlangen, und dessen, was wir von dem, was sie sehen, verlangen. Wozu dient das Sehen, wenn die wahren Kräfte, die unser Leben bestimmen, unsichtbar geworden sind? Bietet die Bildwelt Erkenntnis oder Ablenkung? …

… *Lichts Wahrheit.* Die Ungläubigen werden hingegen *in der Finsternis verbannt.* Und versteht man etwas, dann sieht man, was der andere meint. Ein Neugeborenes empfängt über die Augen mehr Reize als über jeden anderen Körperteil mit Ausnahme des Mundes. Auch der Fotograf Walker Evans bezog sich …

… ausgesetzt ist, doch visuelle Stimuli lassen noch mit verstehen, obwohl sie für beides eine Rolle spielen kann. Die Angst, dass die Welt der Bilder die bürgerliche Gesellschaft stören oder gar verfälschen könnte, ist vertraut. Wie oft hören wir, dass Bilder uns »bombardieren« …

… nicht erzählen, wem sie gehört oder wie viel derjenige verdient, der sie bedient, oder wie viel Gewinn sie erwirtschaftet. Zu einem späteren Zeitpunkt sagen wir, in den Jahren nach dem Zweiten Weltkrieg verkomplizierte sich diese Welt der Maschinen durch die rasche Ausbreitung der elektronischen …

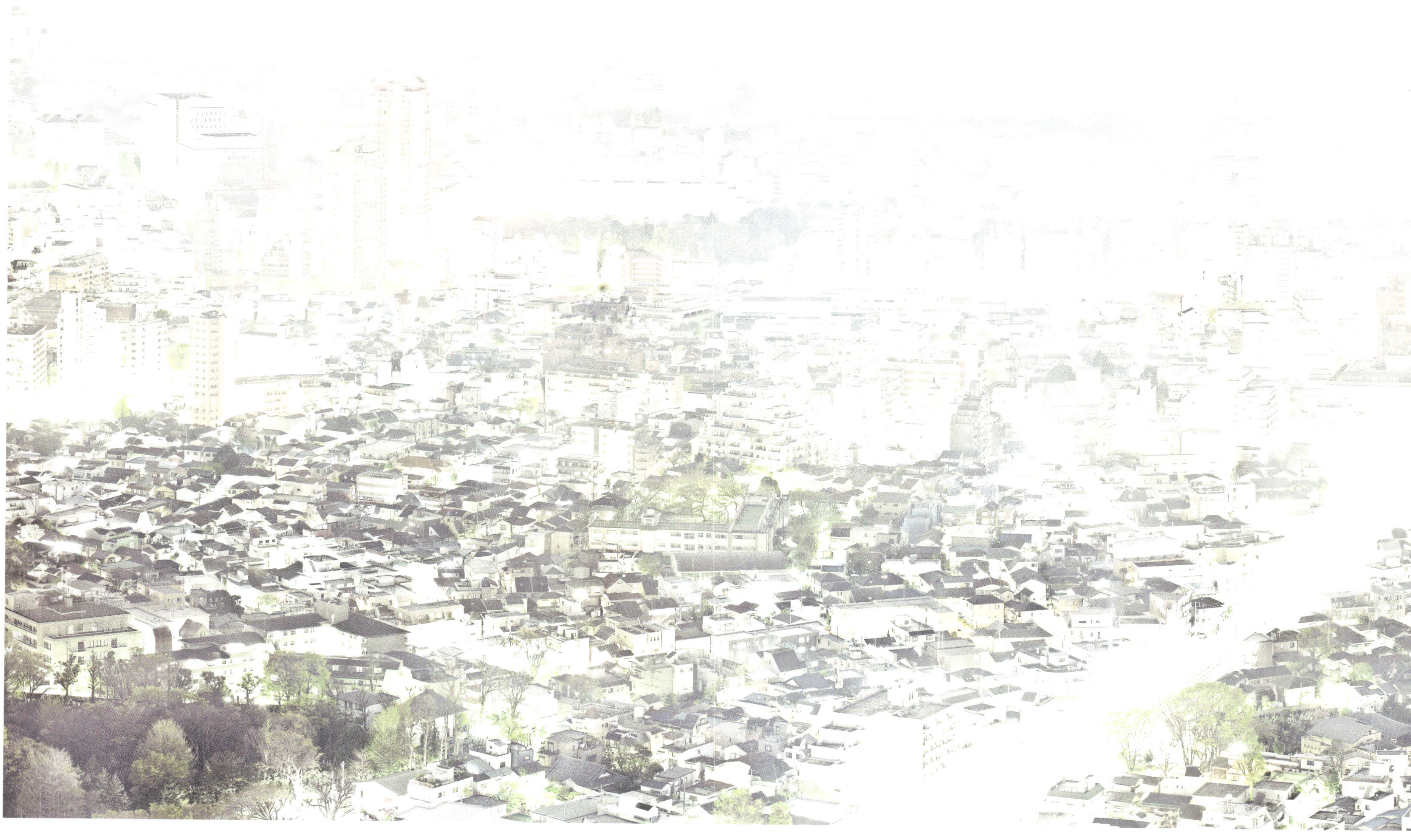

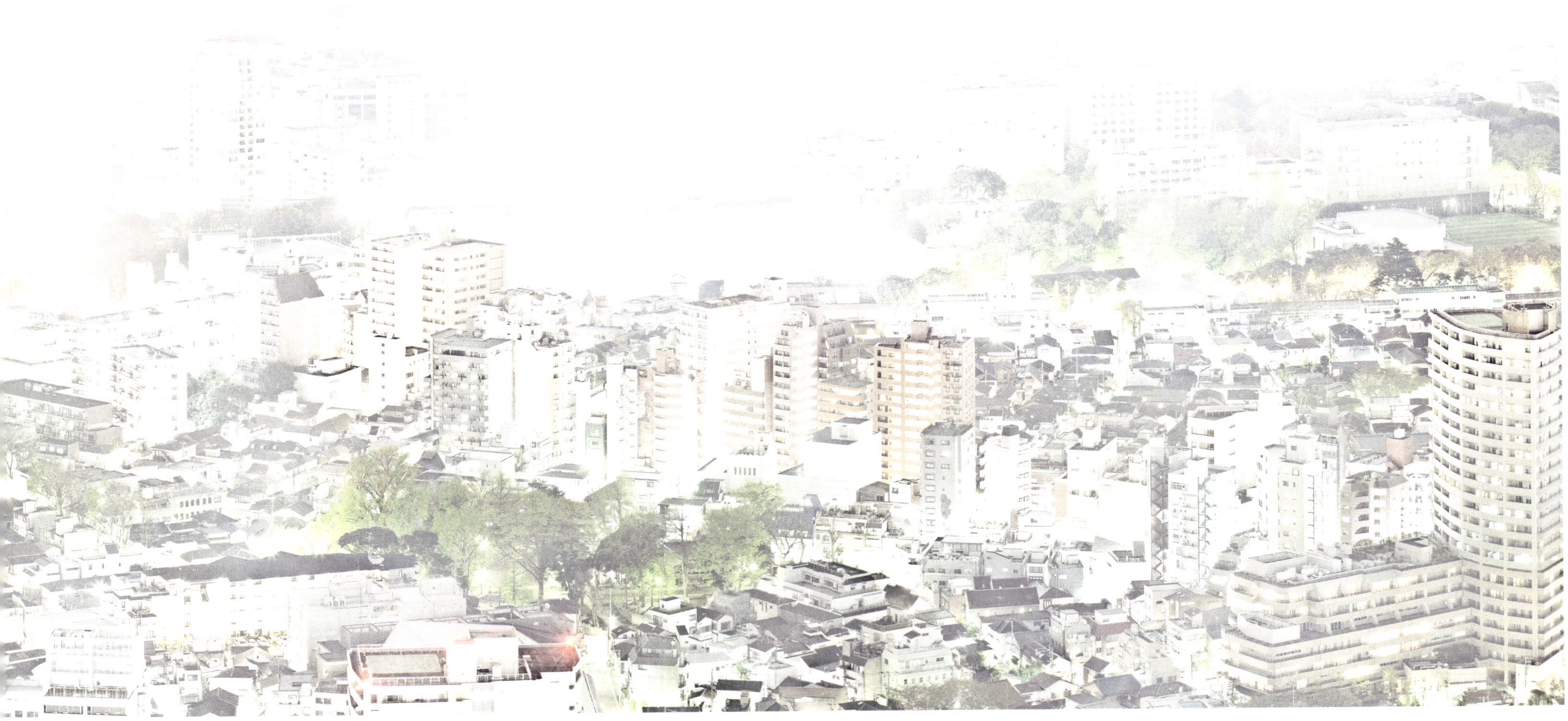

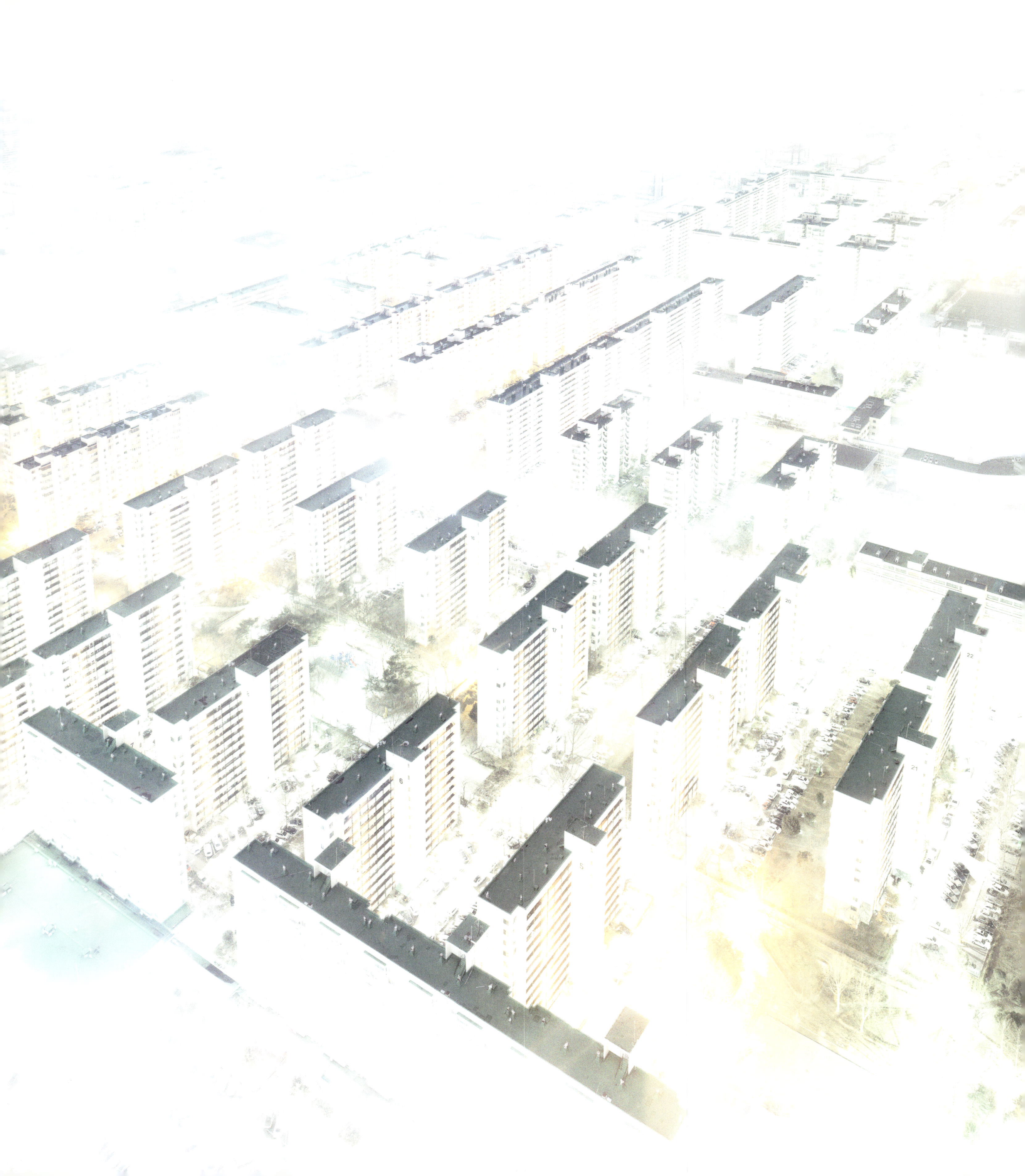

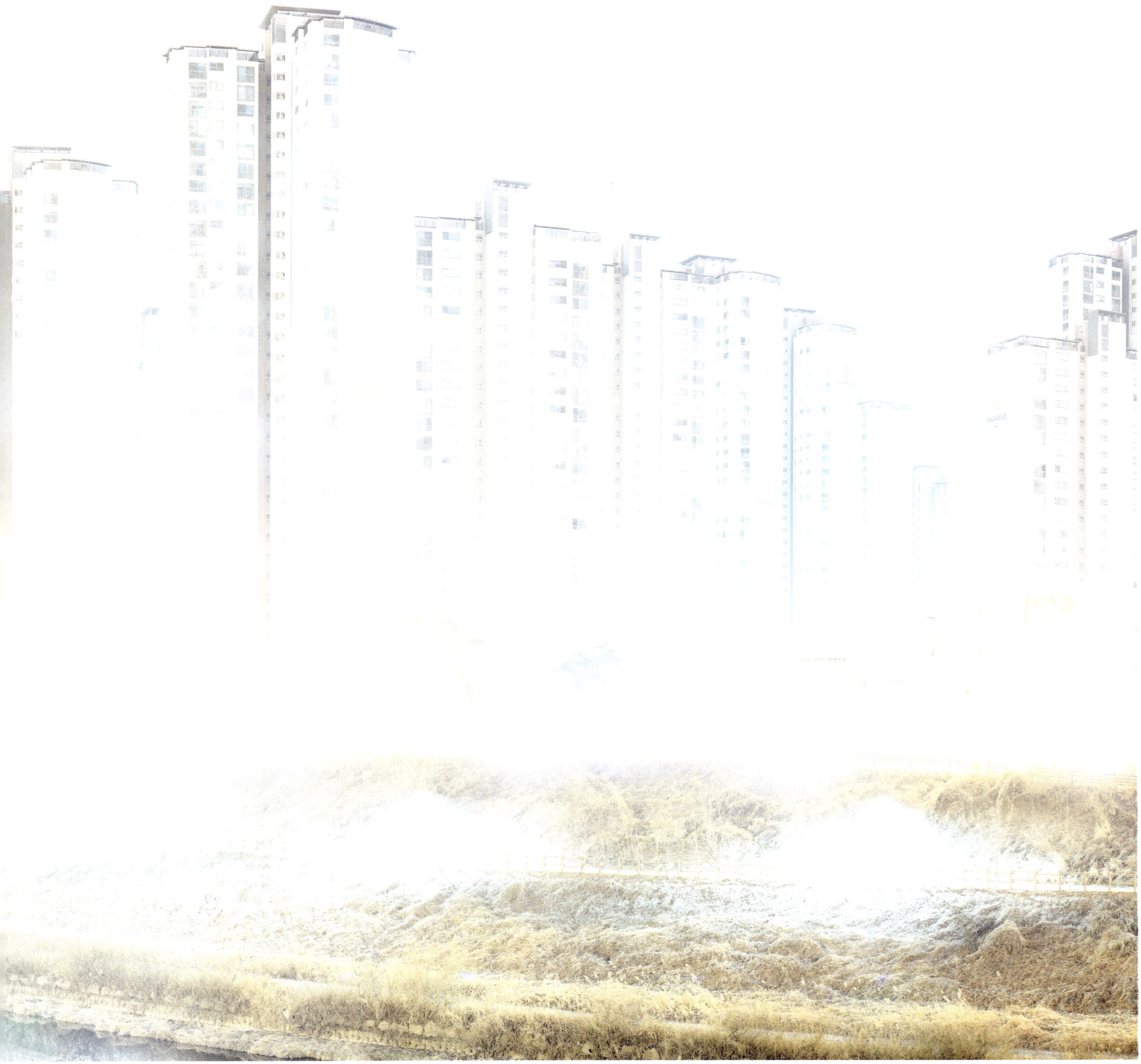

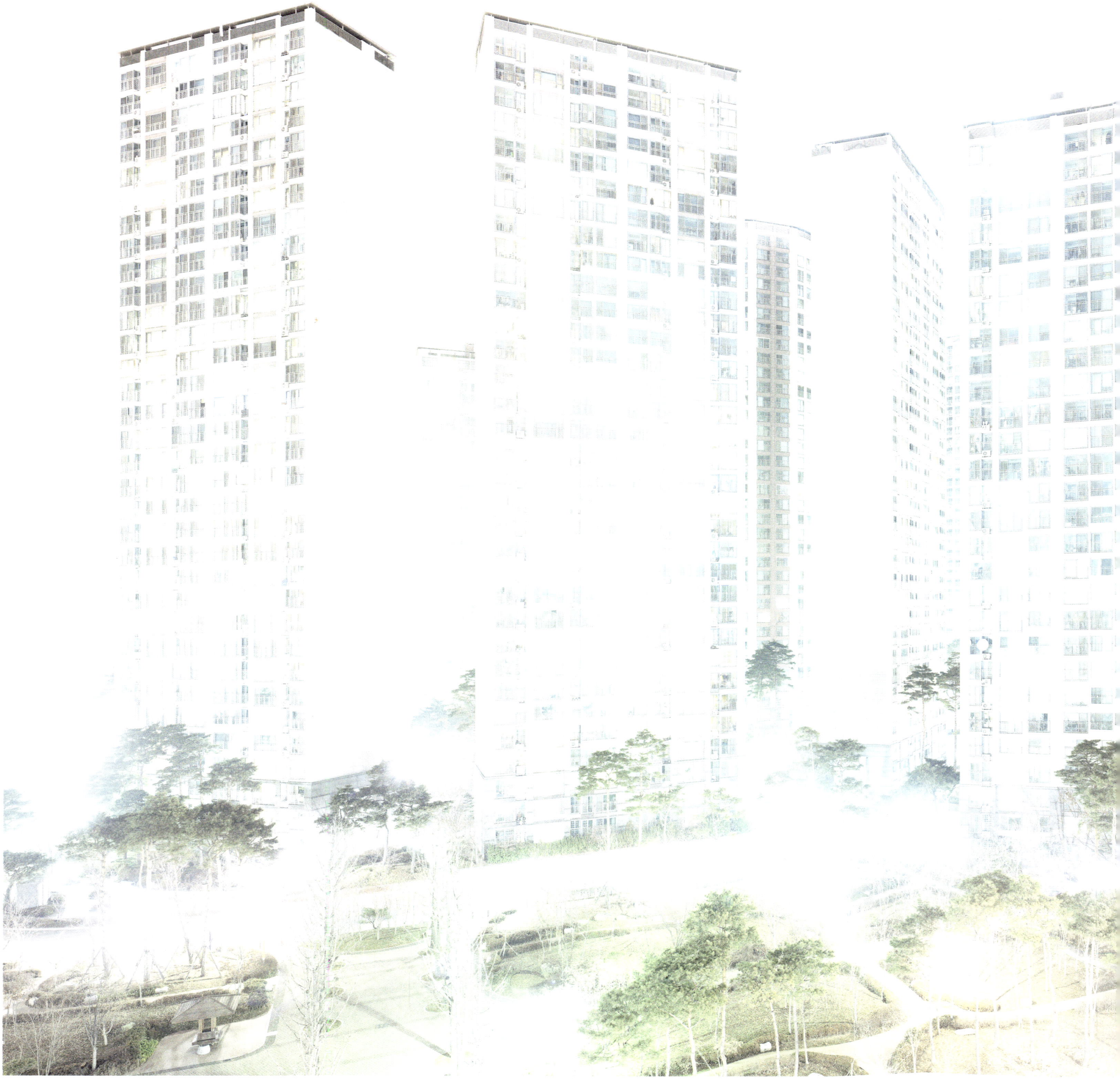

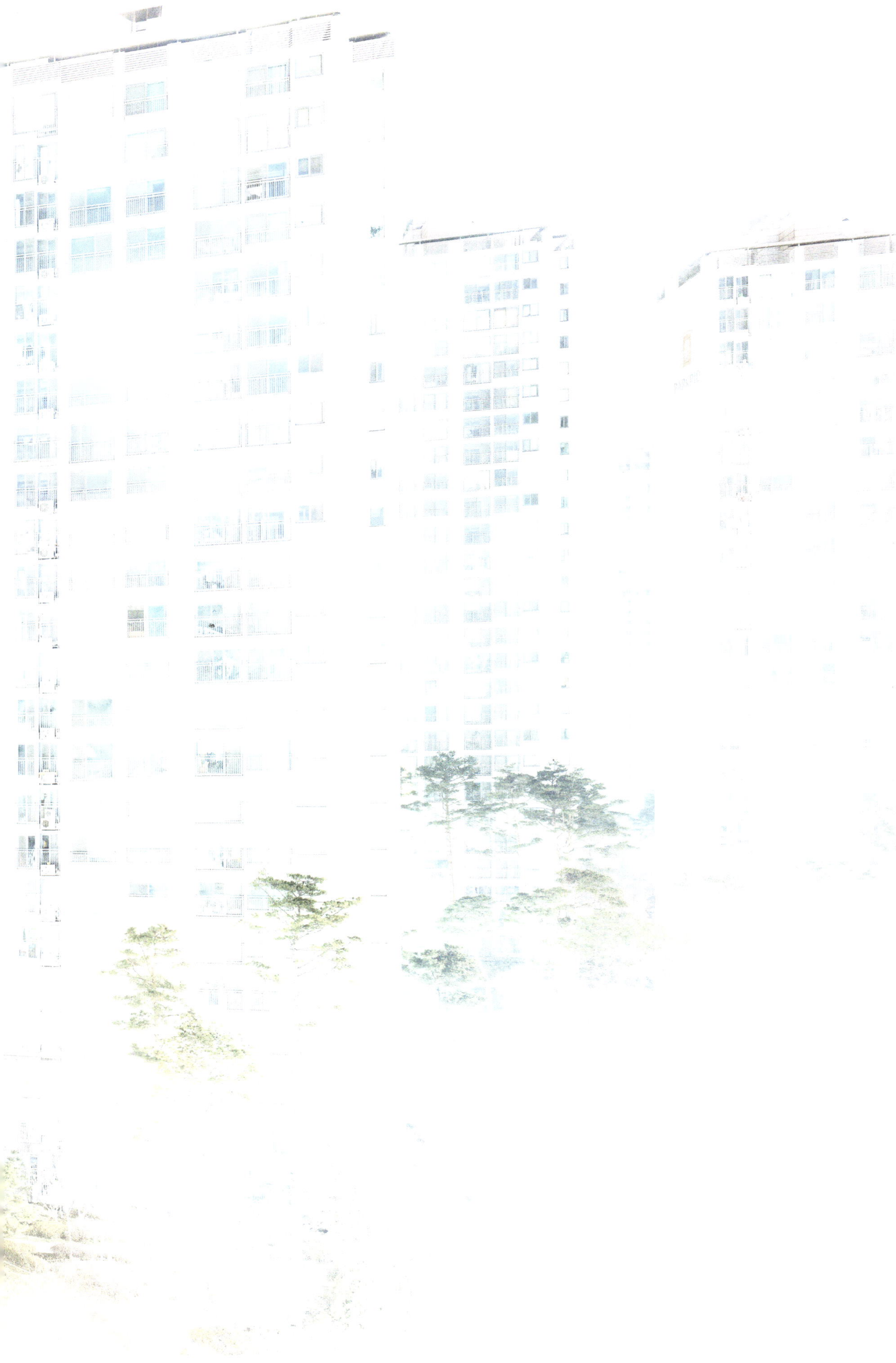

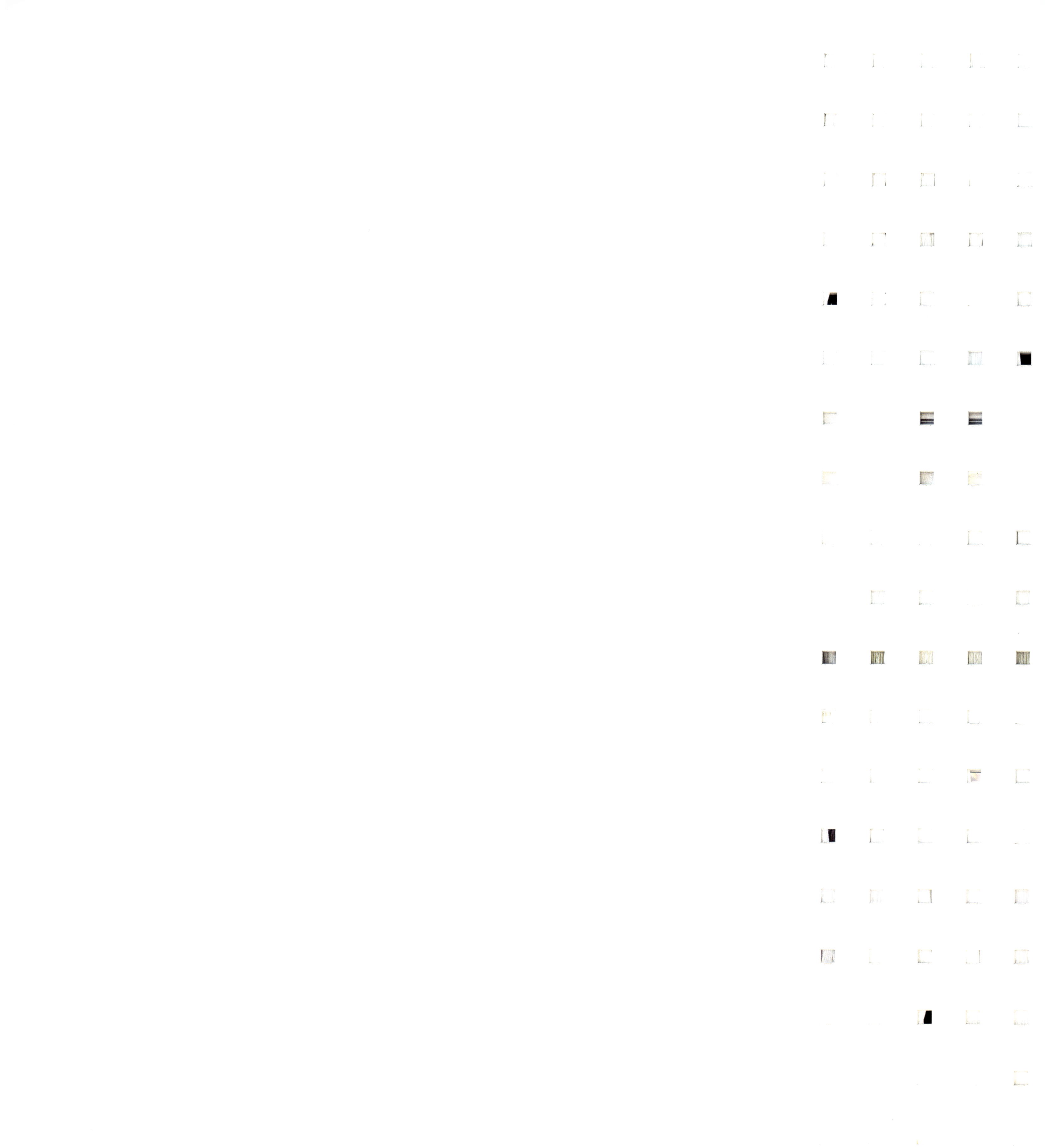

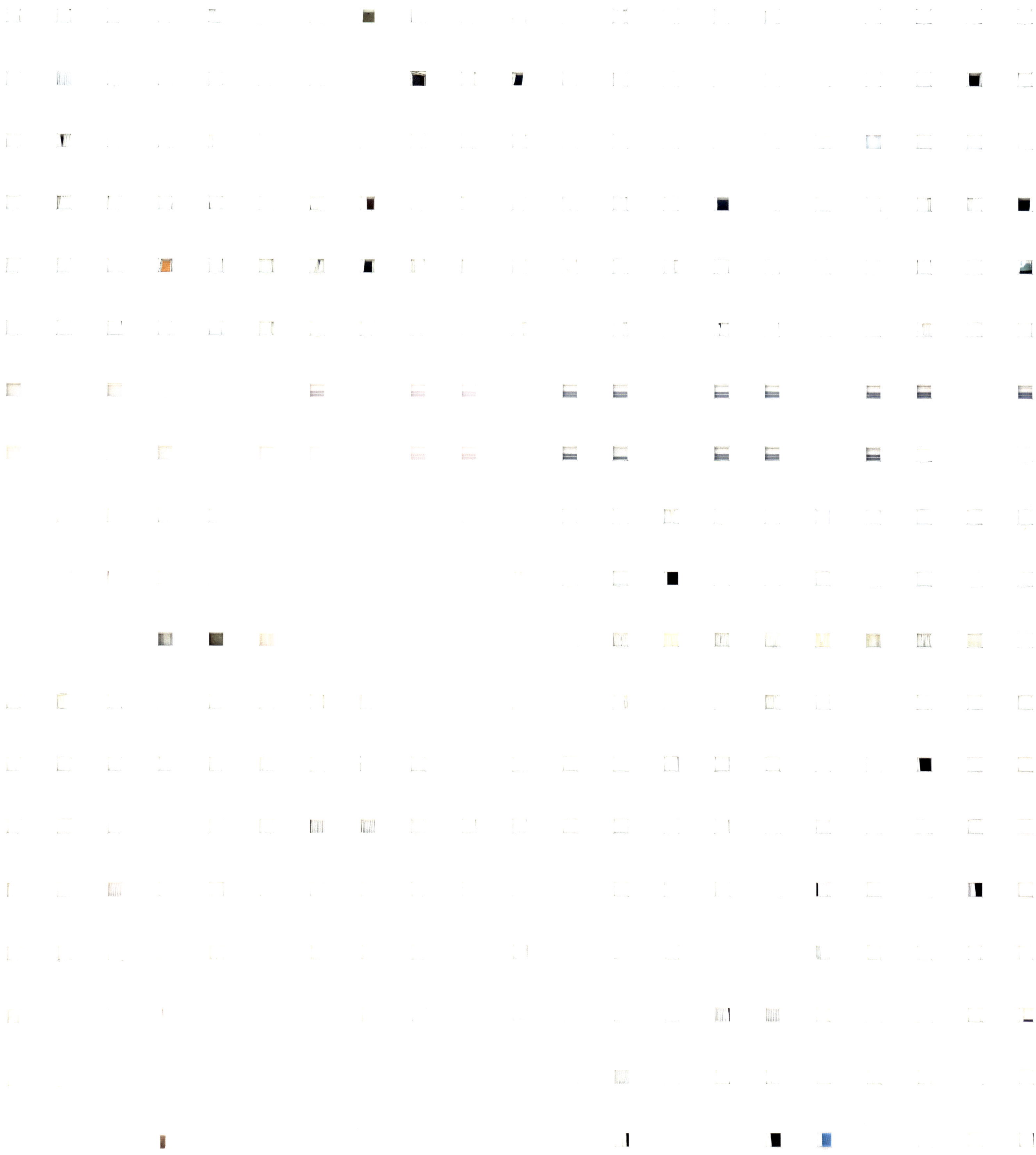

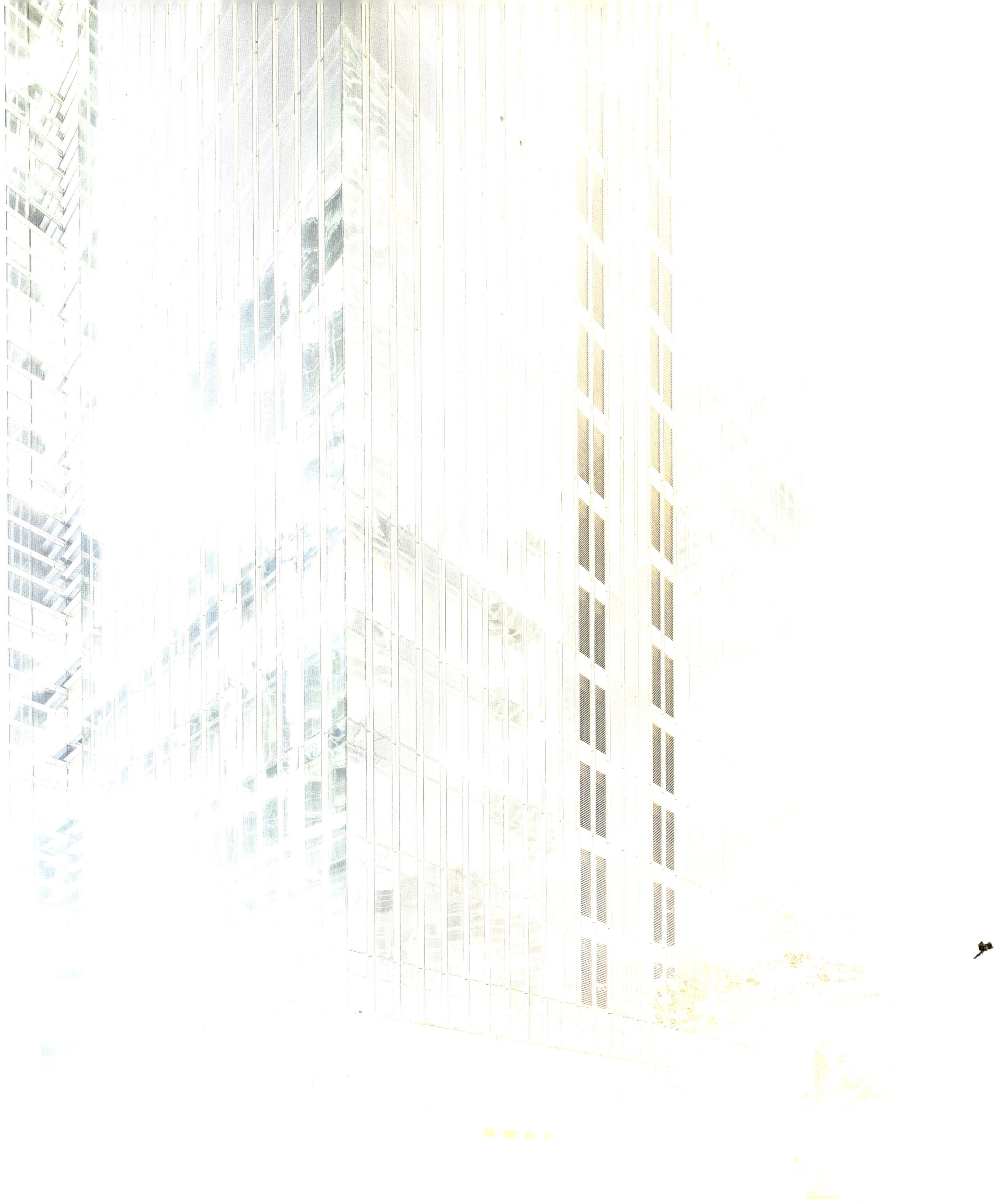

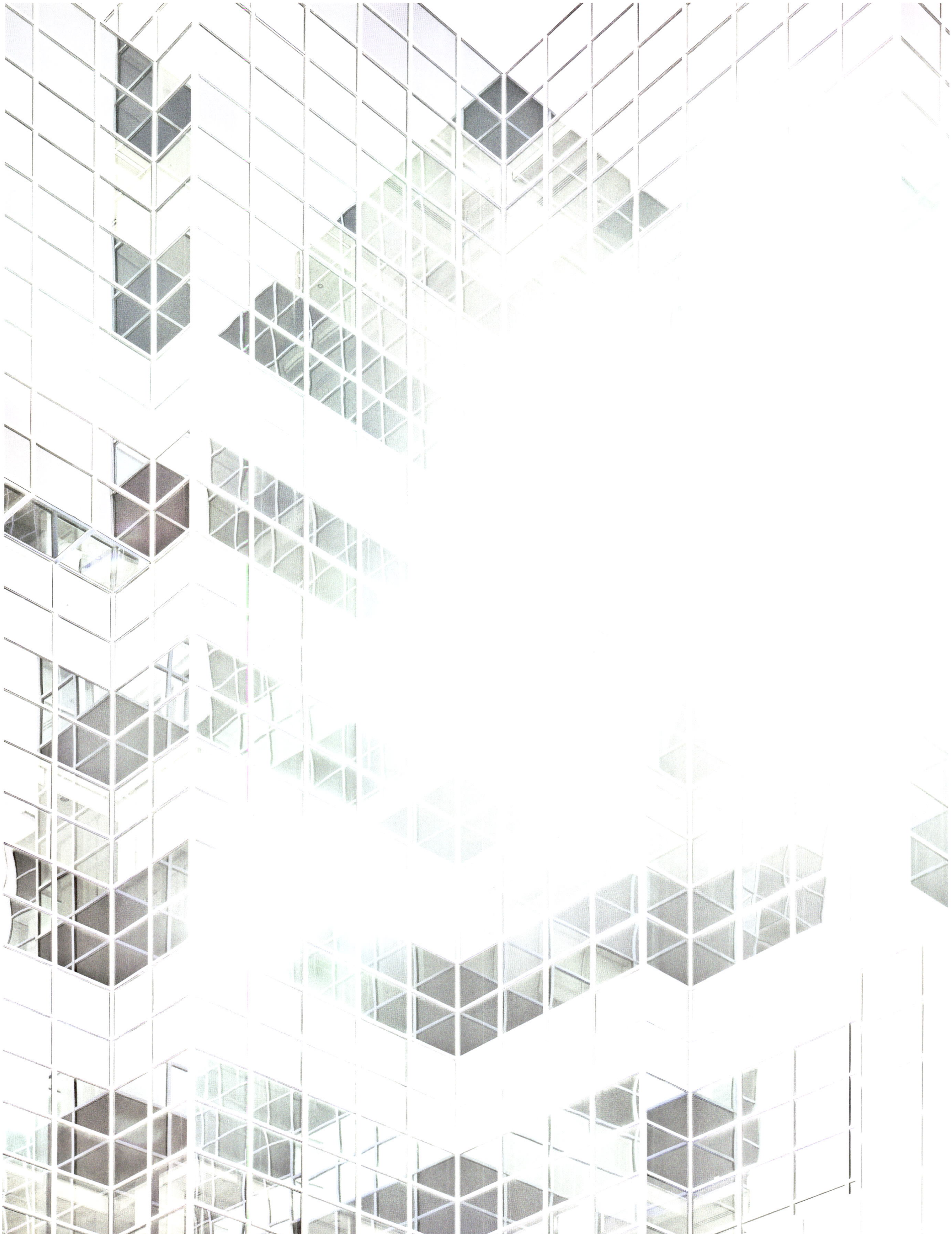

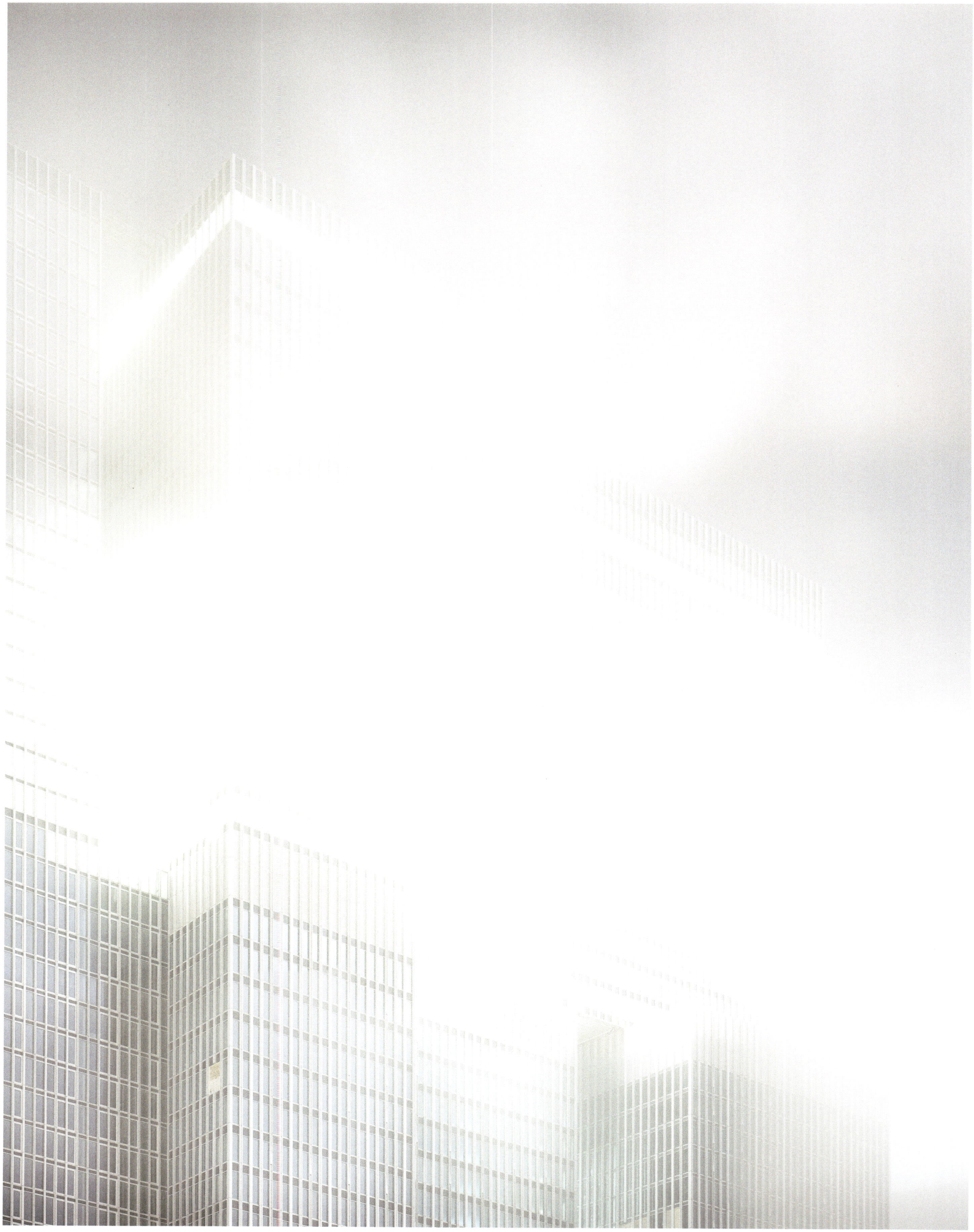

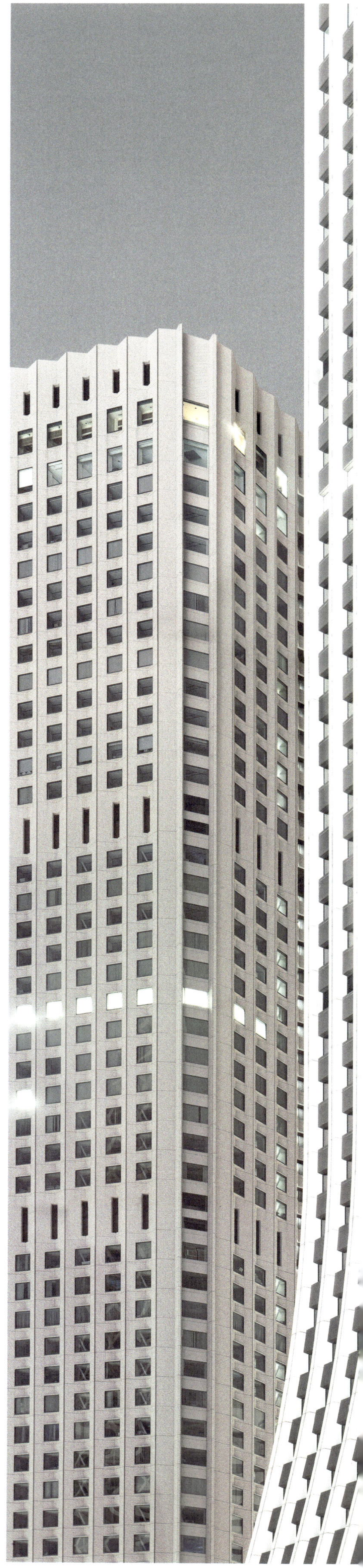

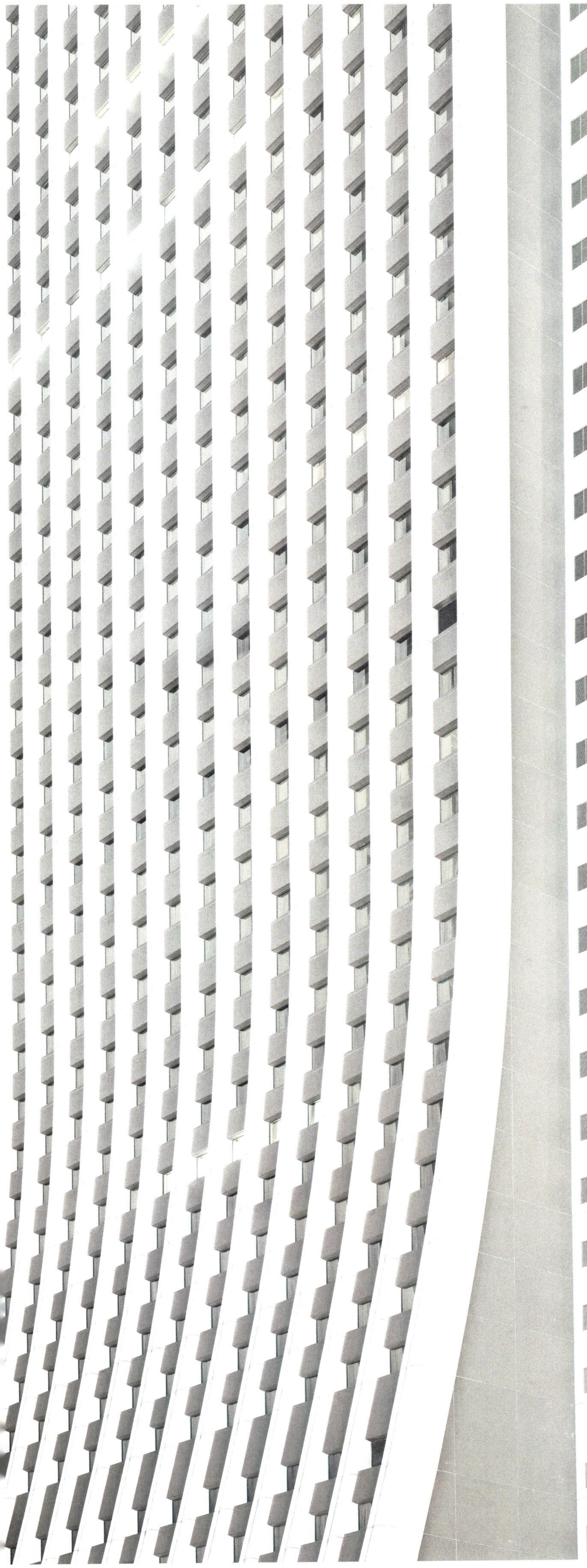
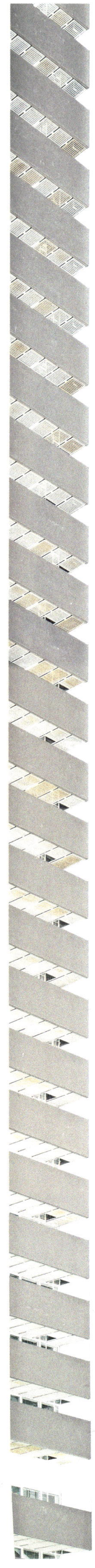

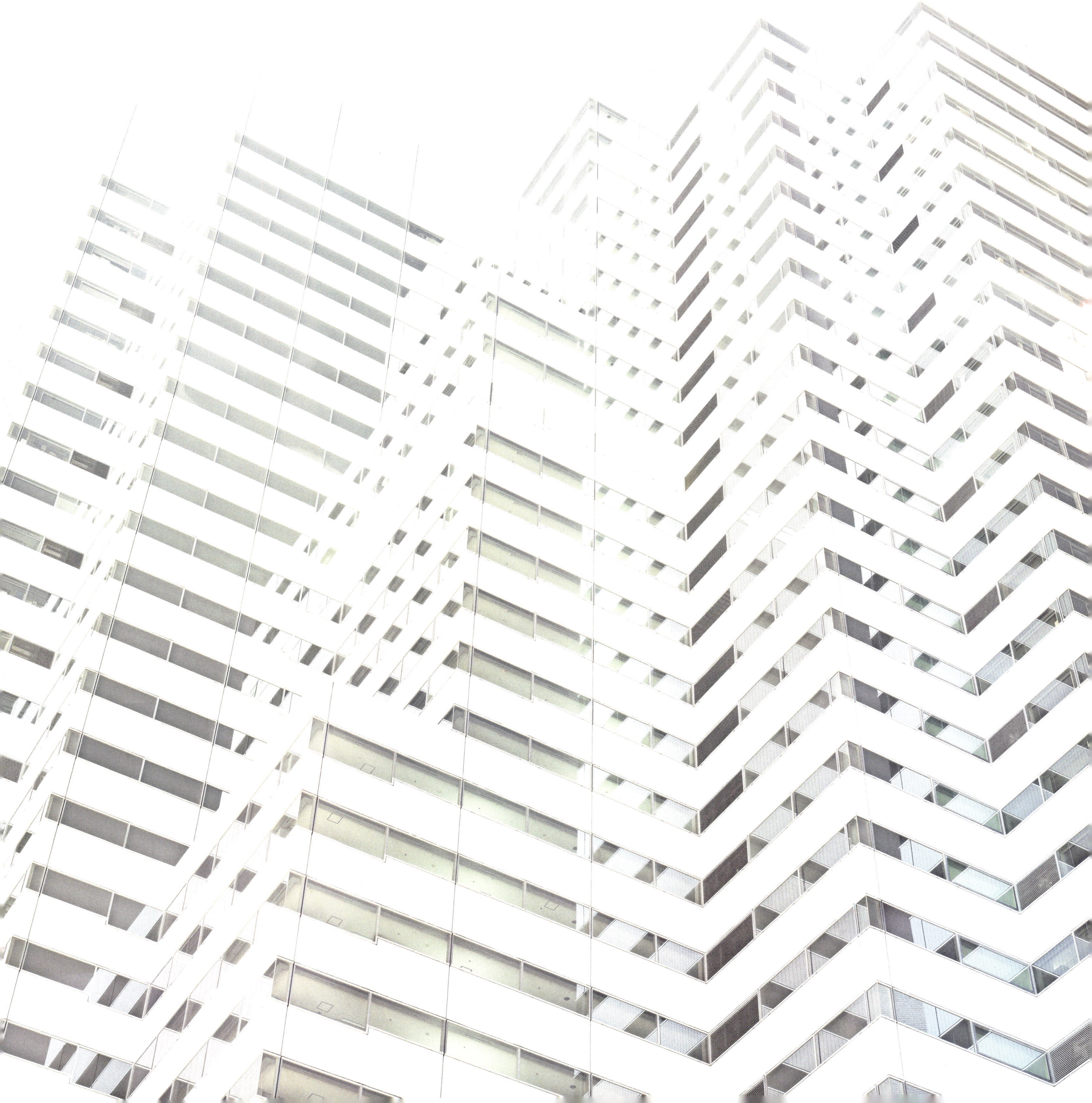

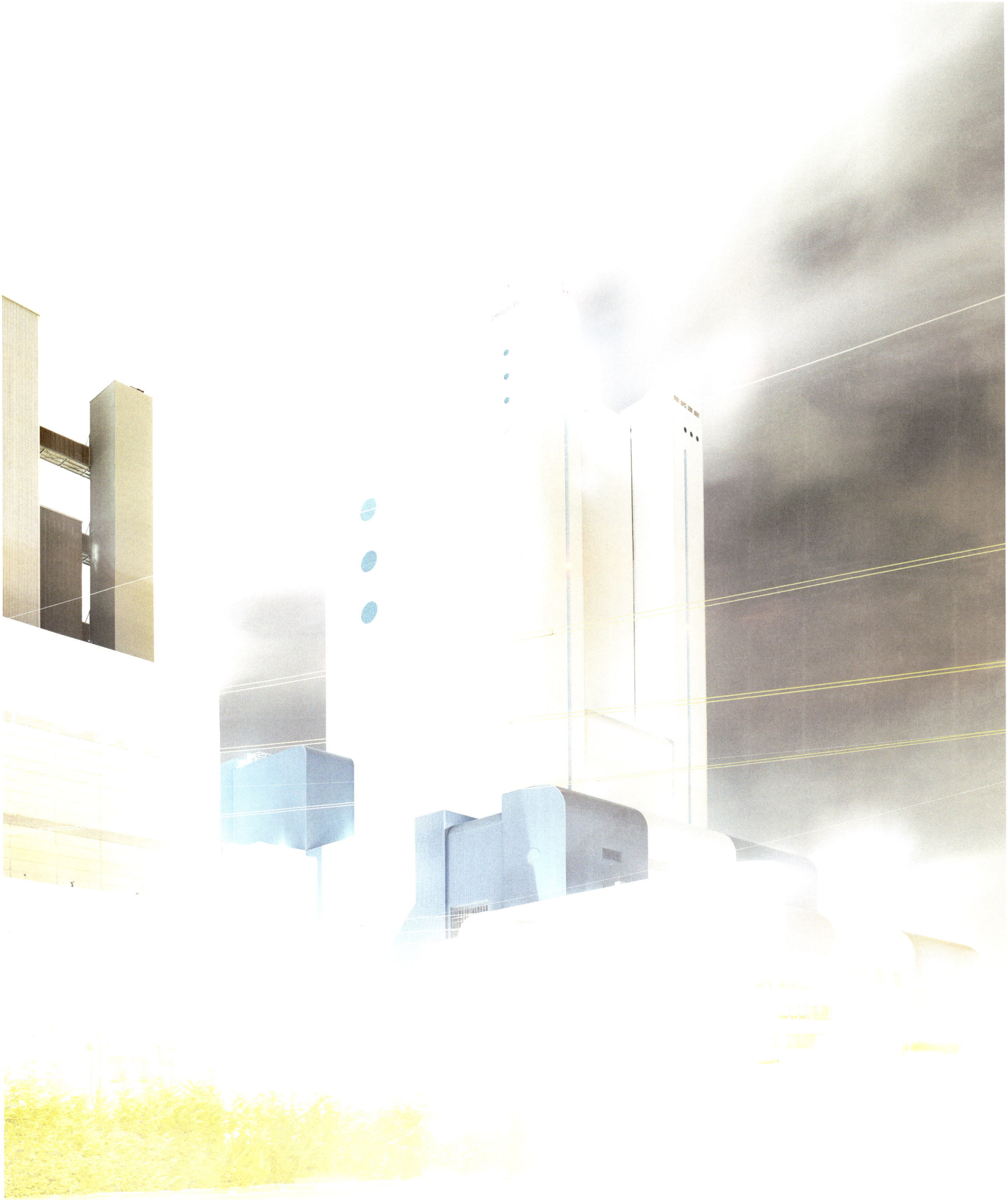

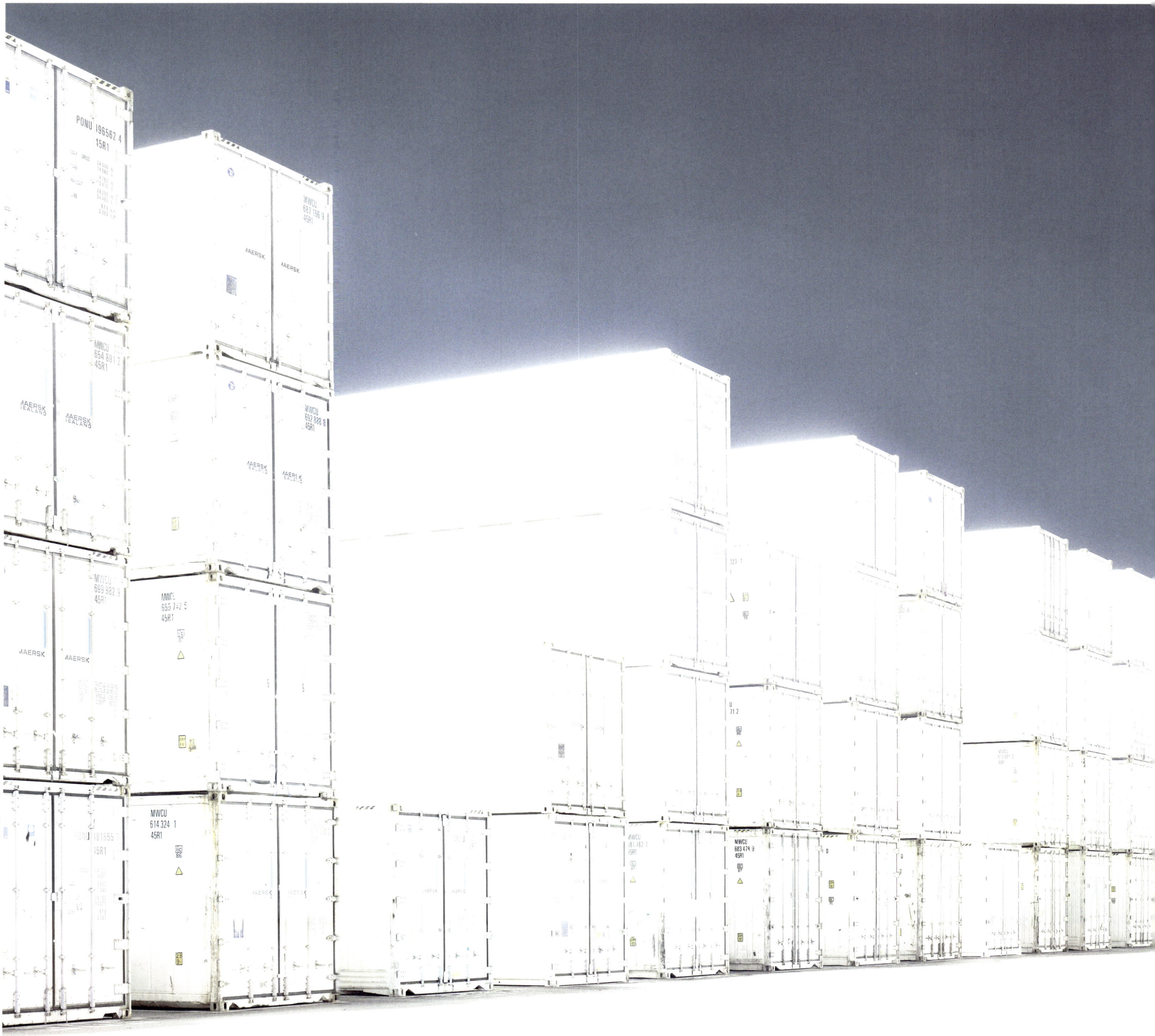
PONU 196562 4
15R1
MWCU
654 891 2
45R1
MAERSK
MWCU
699 982 9
45R1
MAERSK
MWCU
614 324 1
45R1

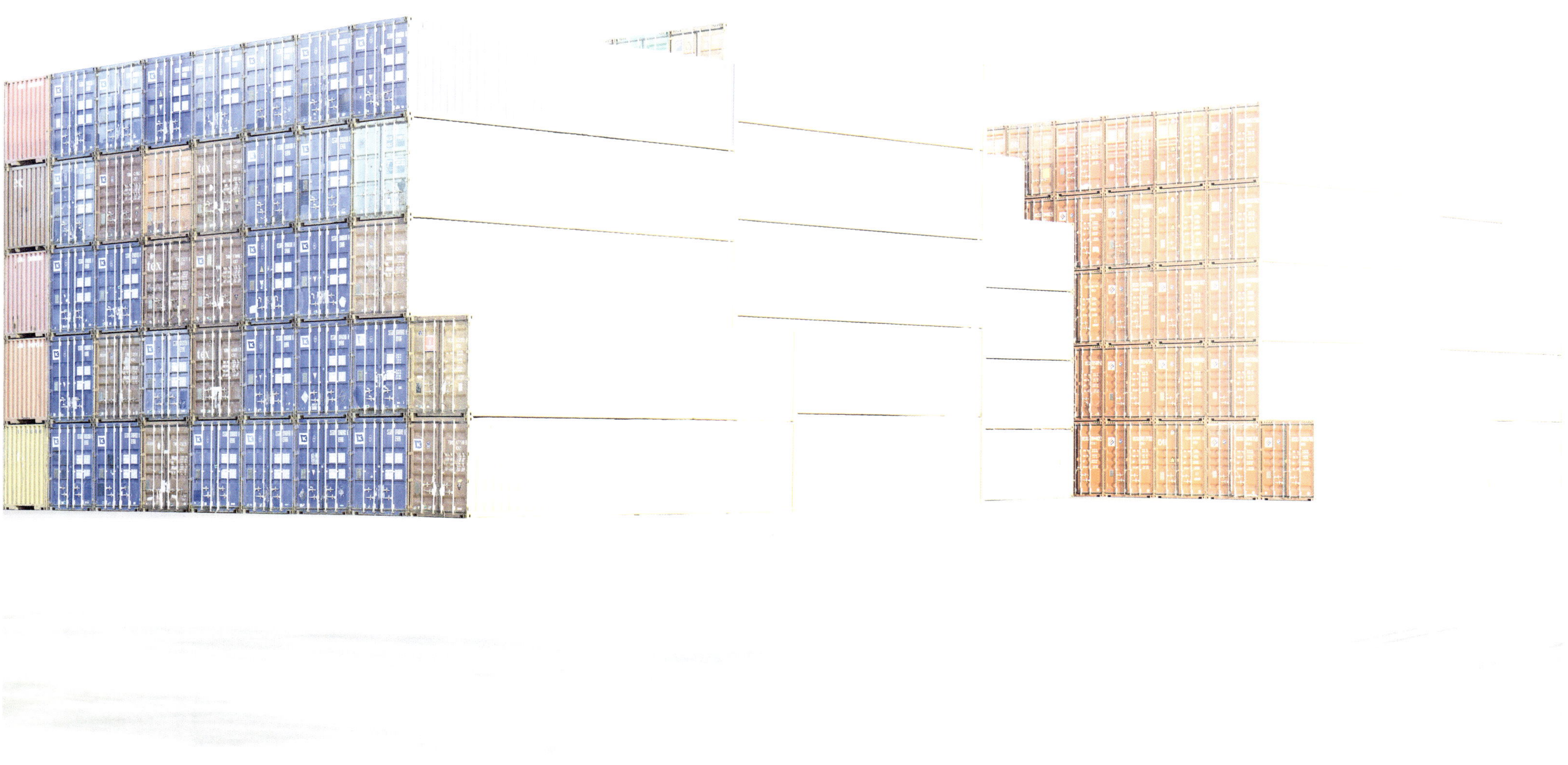

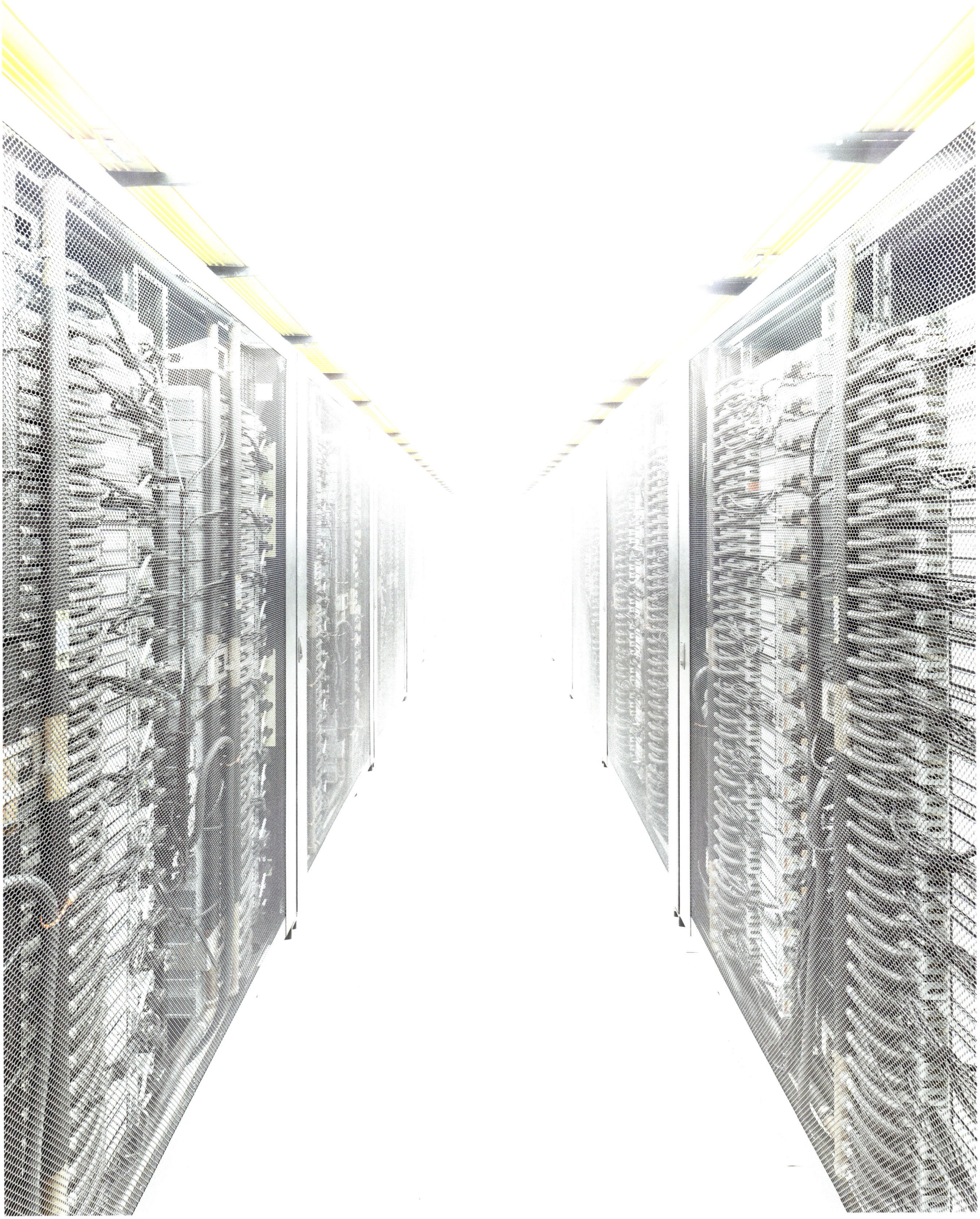

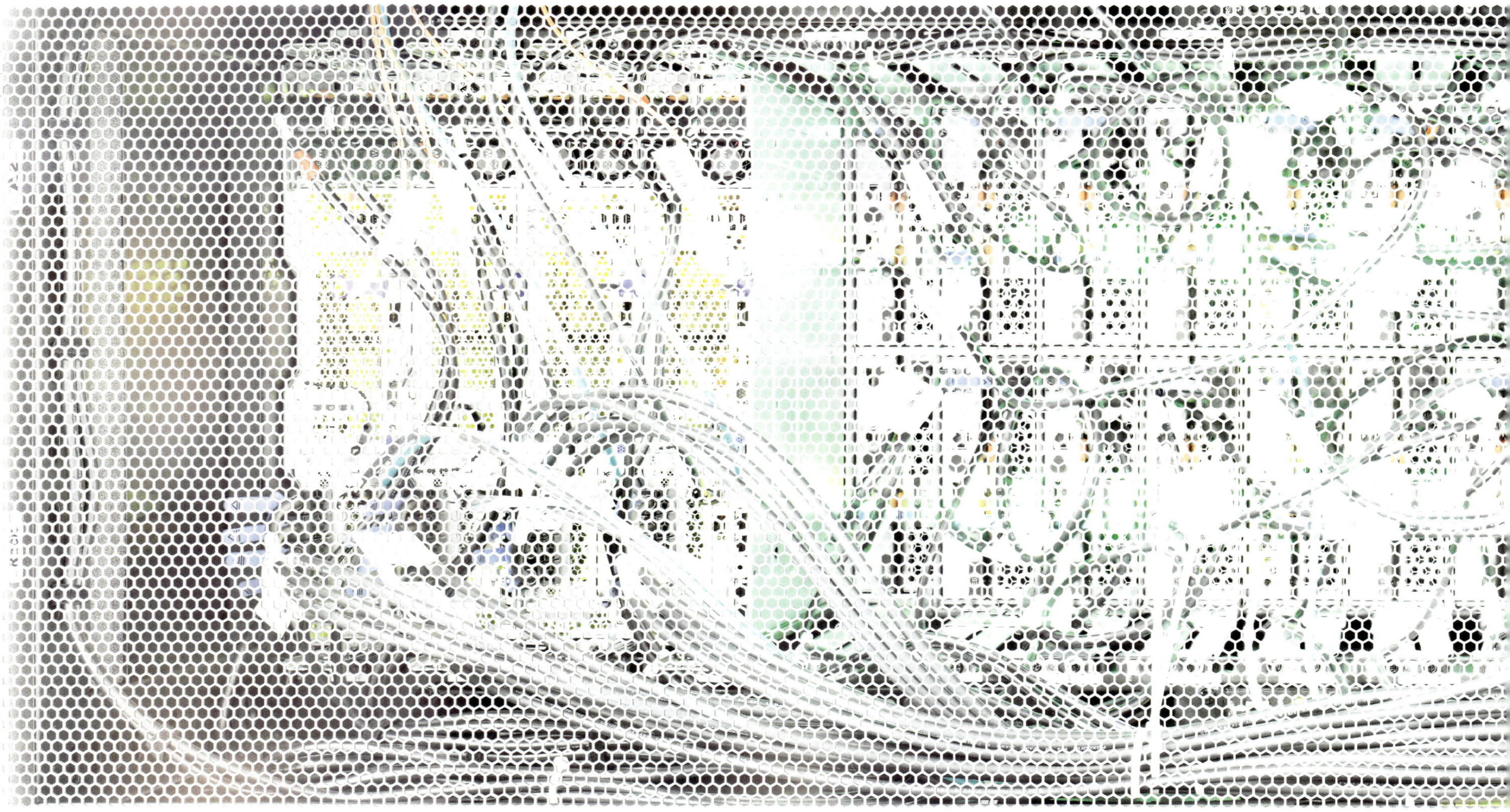

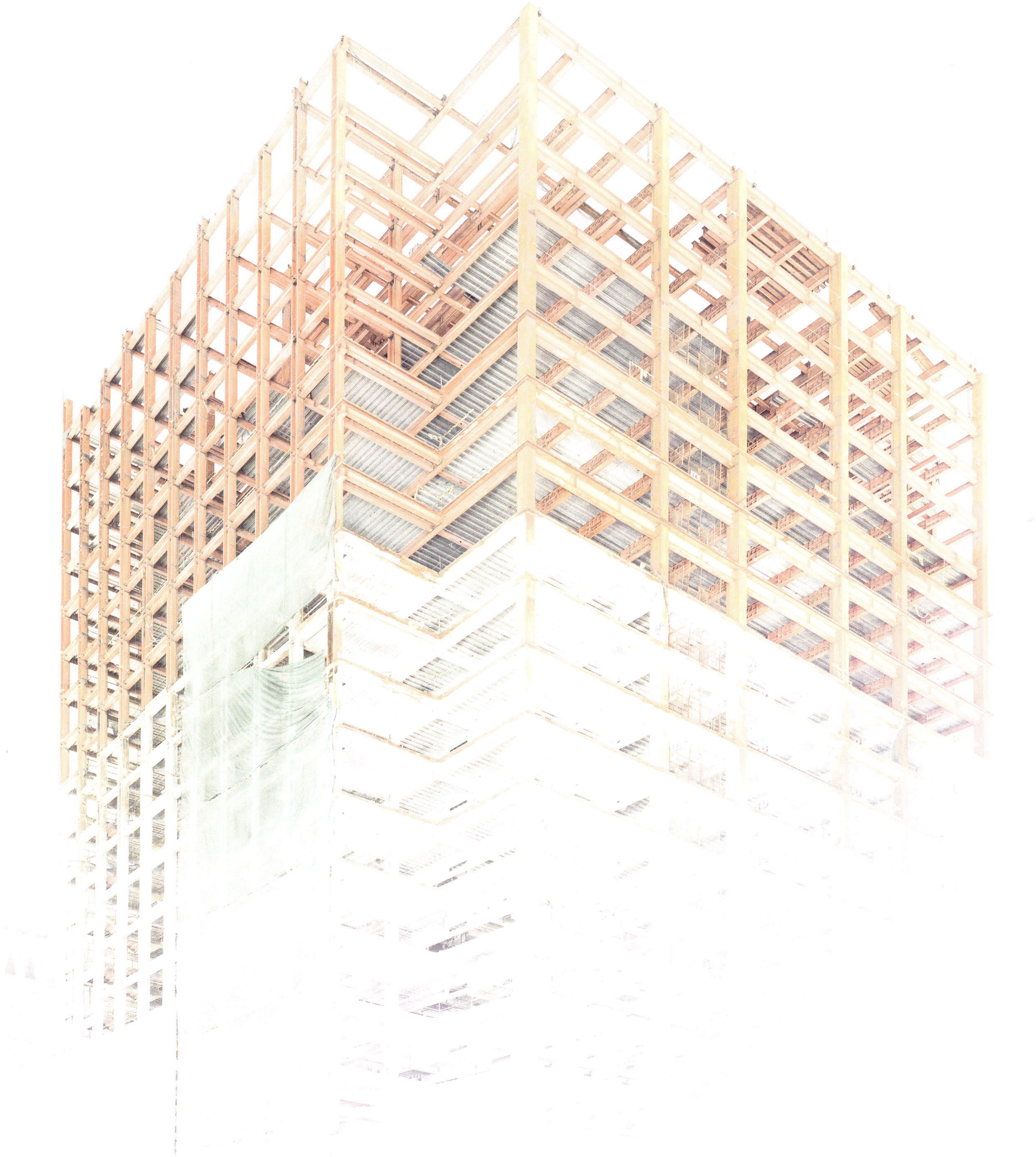

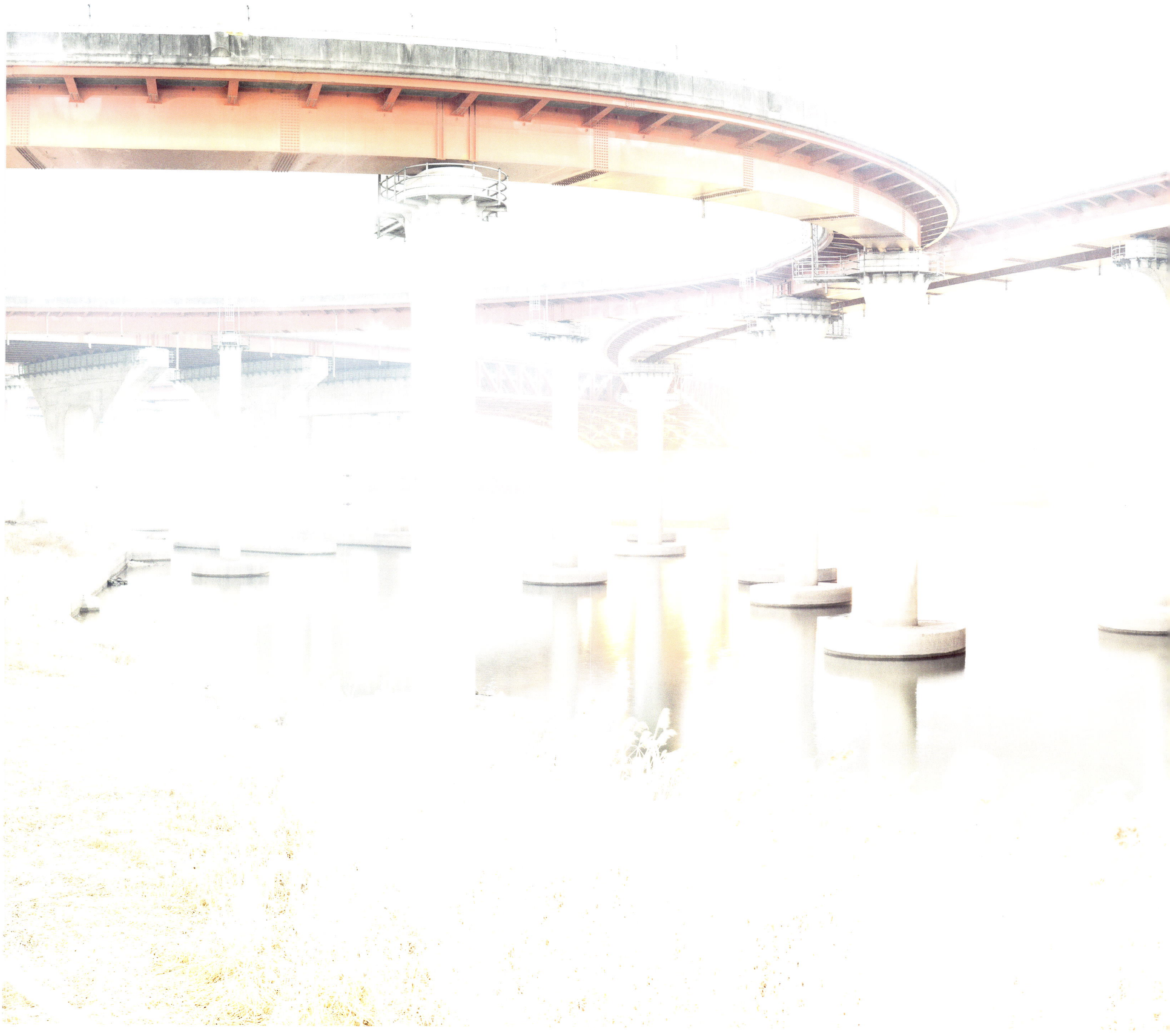

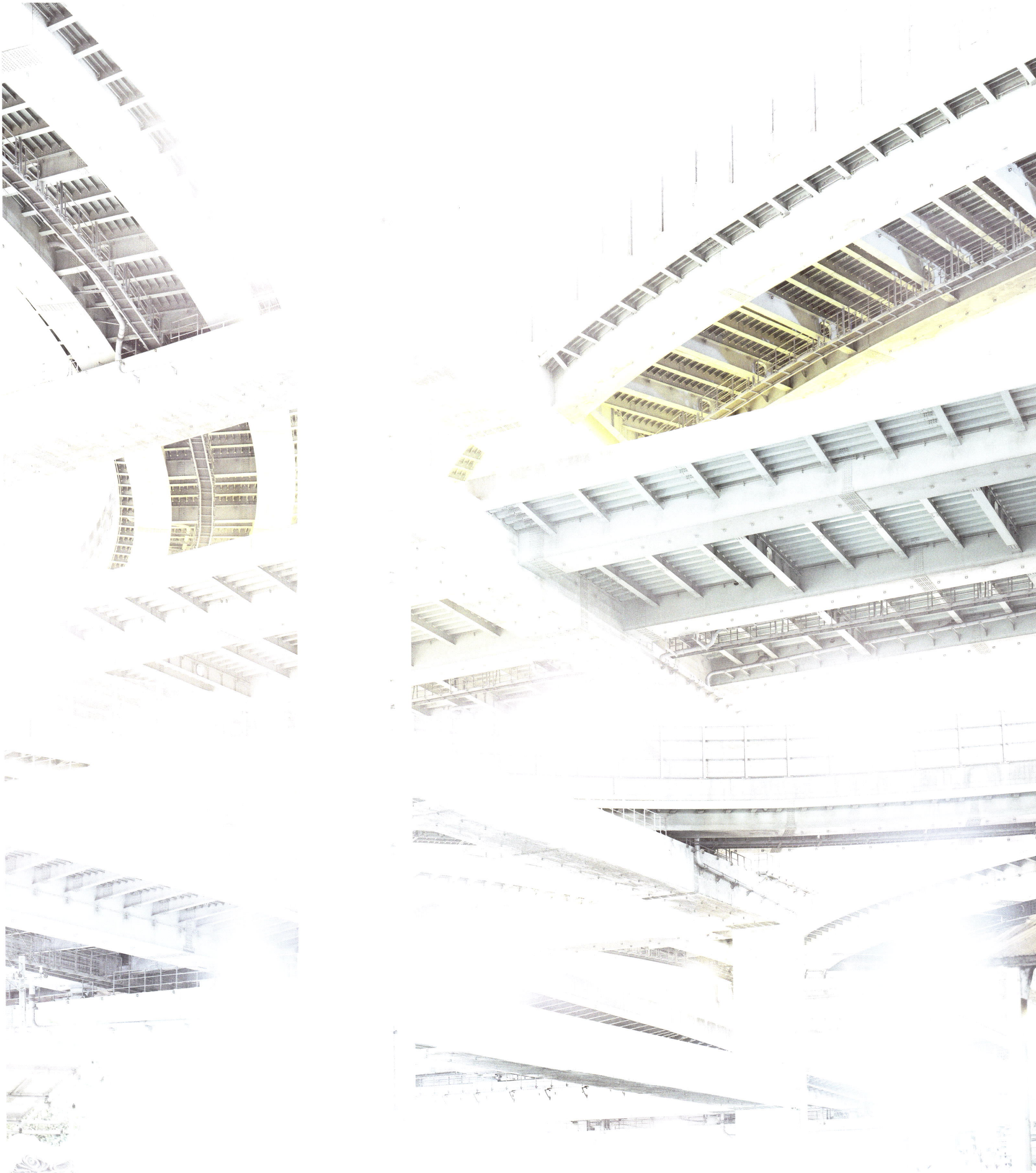

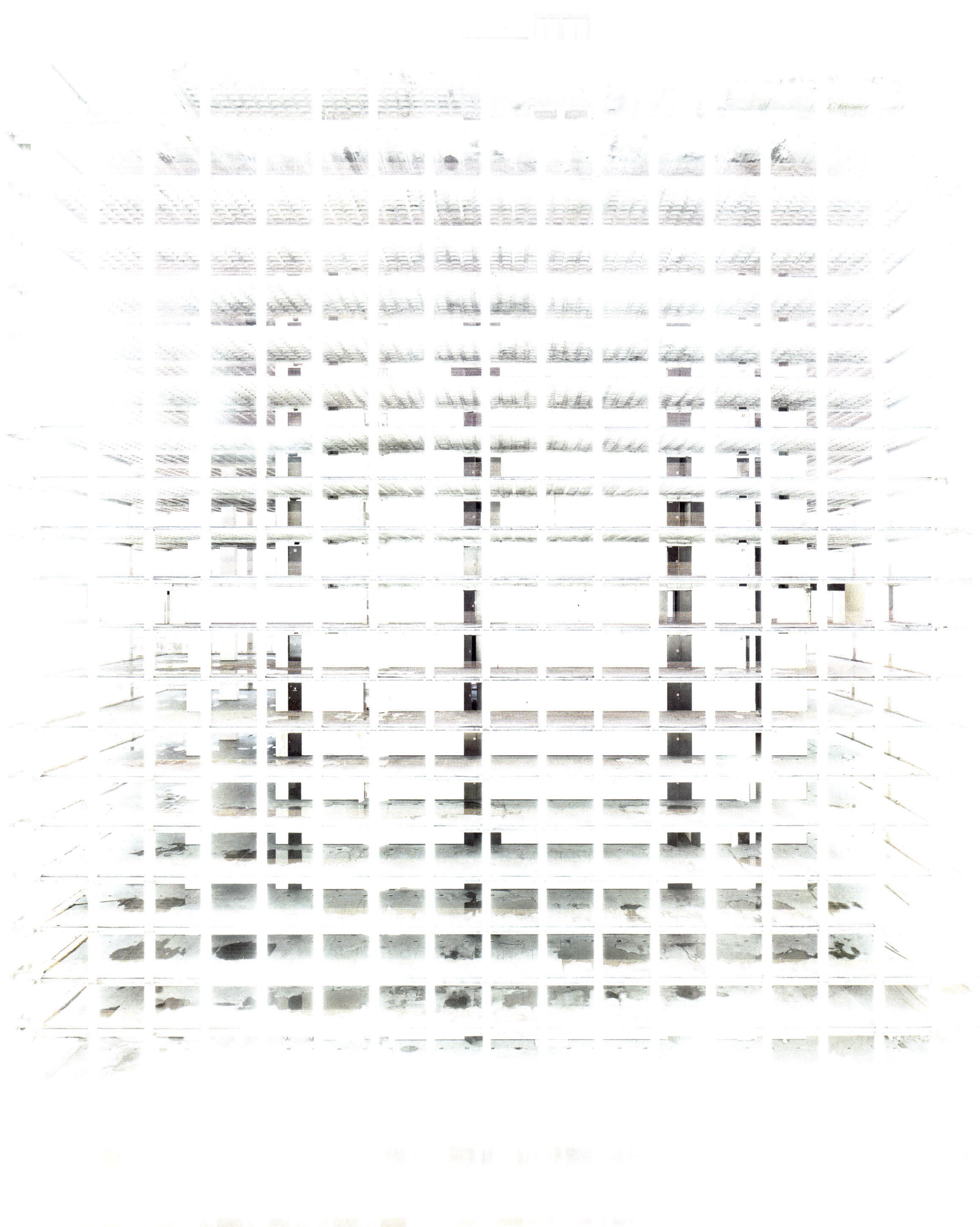

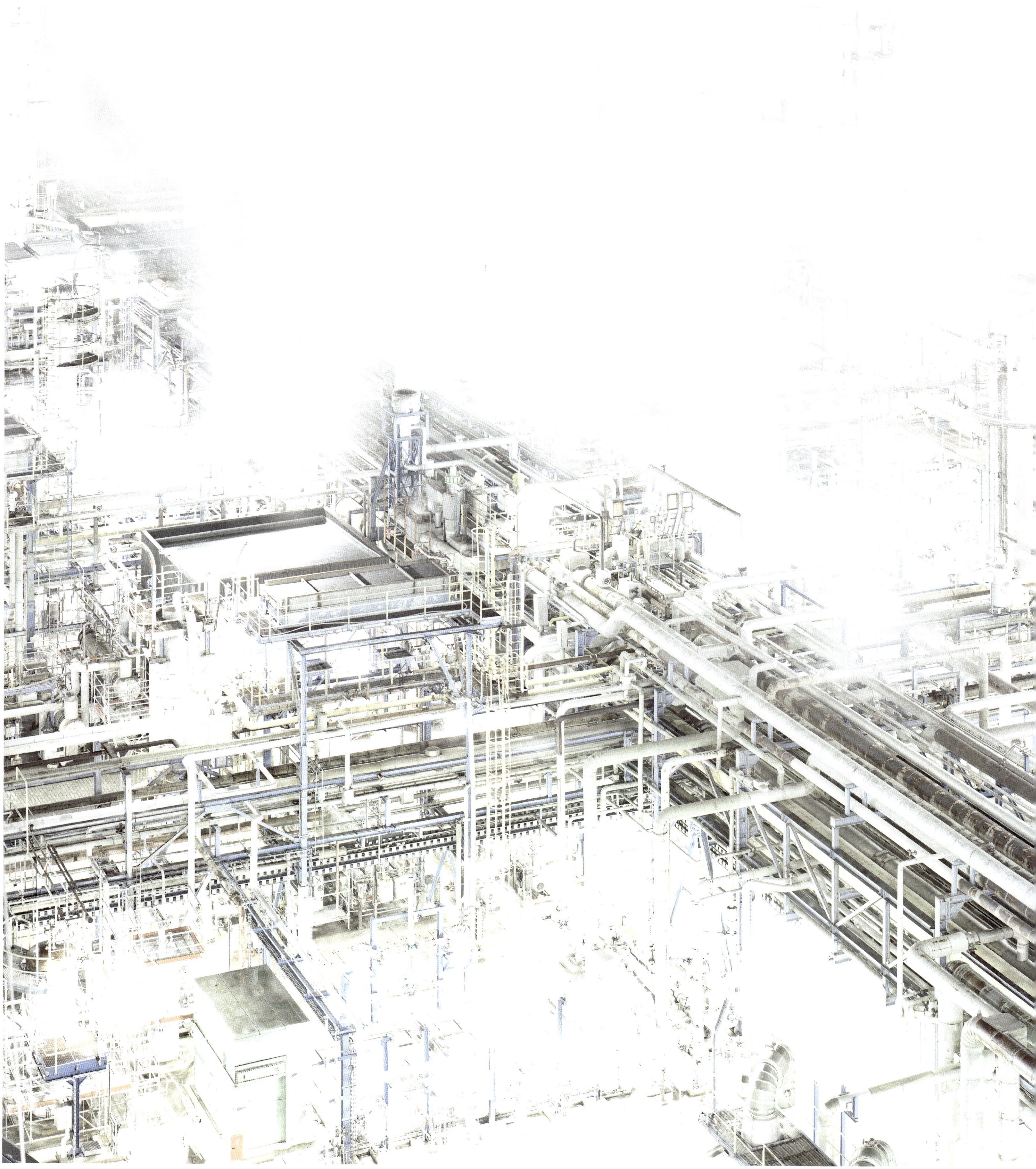

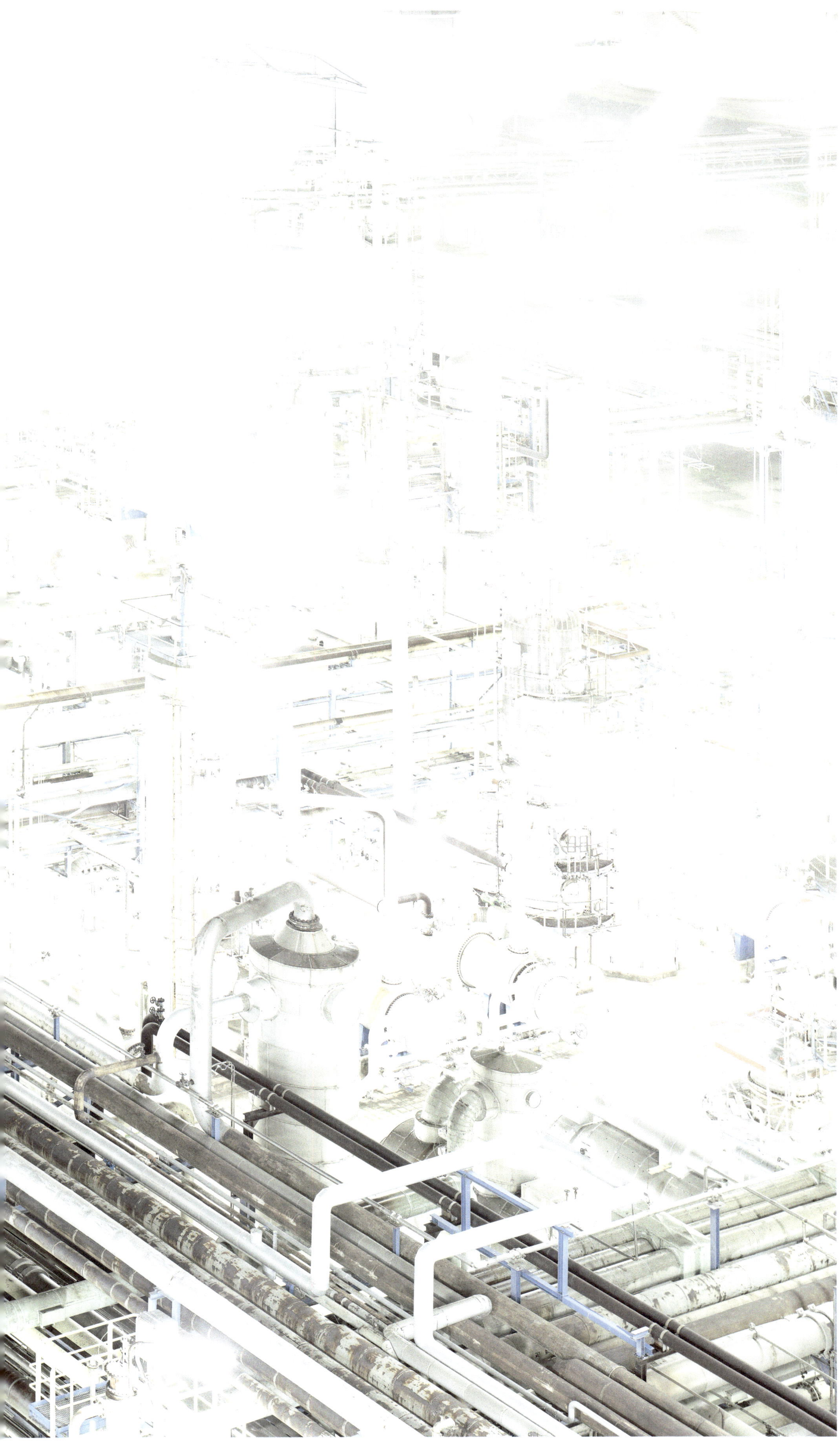

E-4810

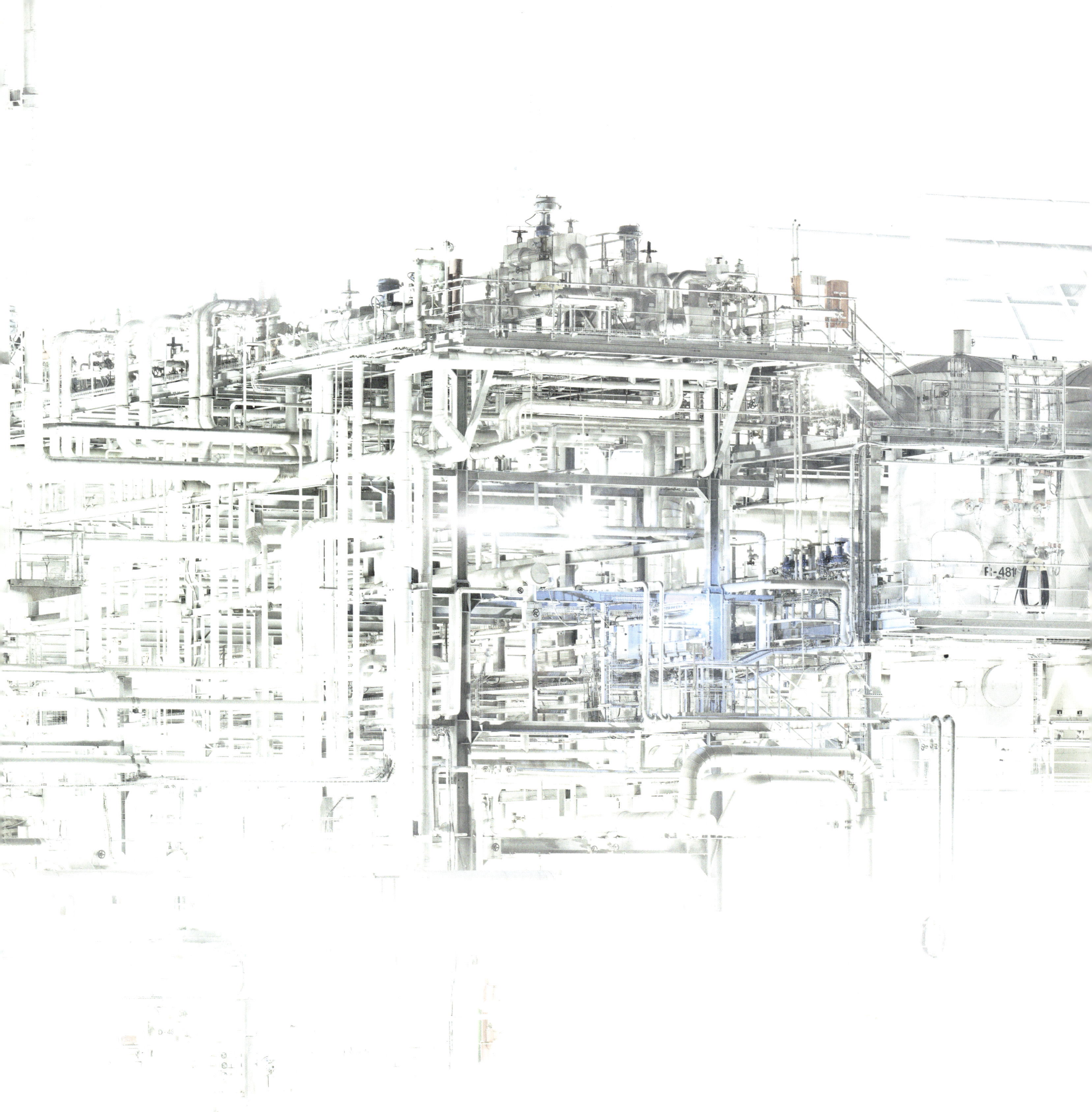

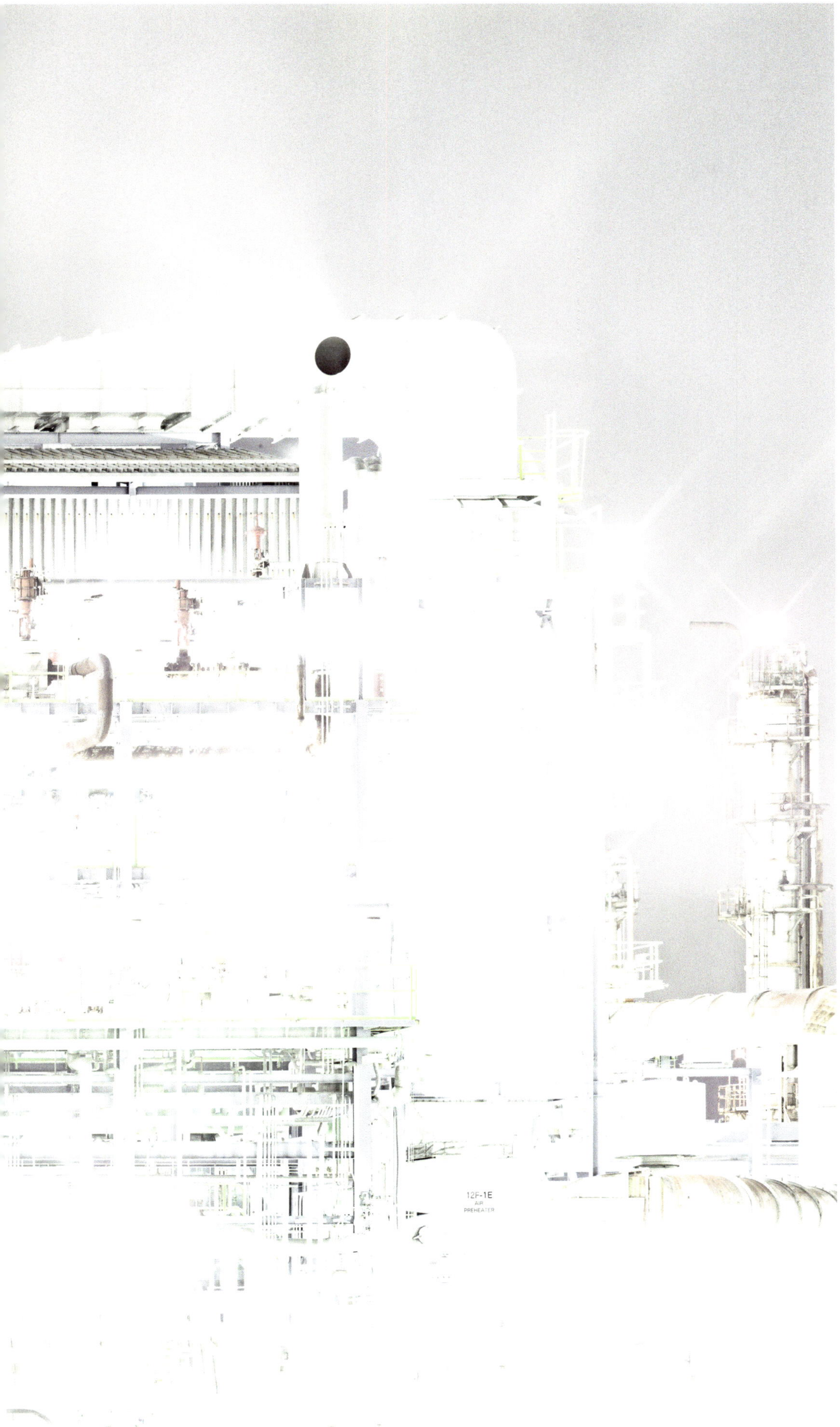
12F-1E
AIR
PREHEATER

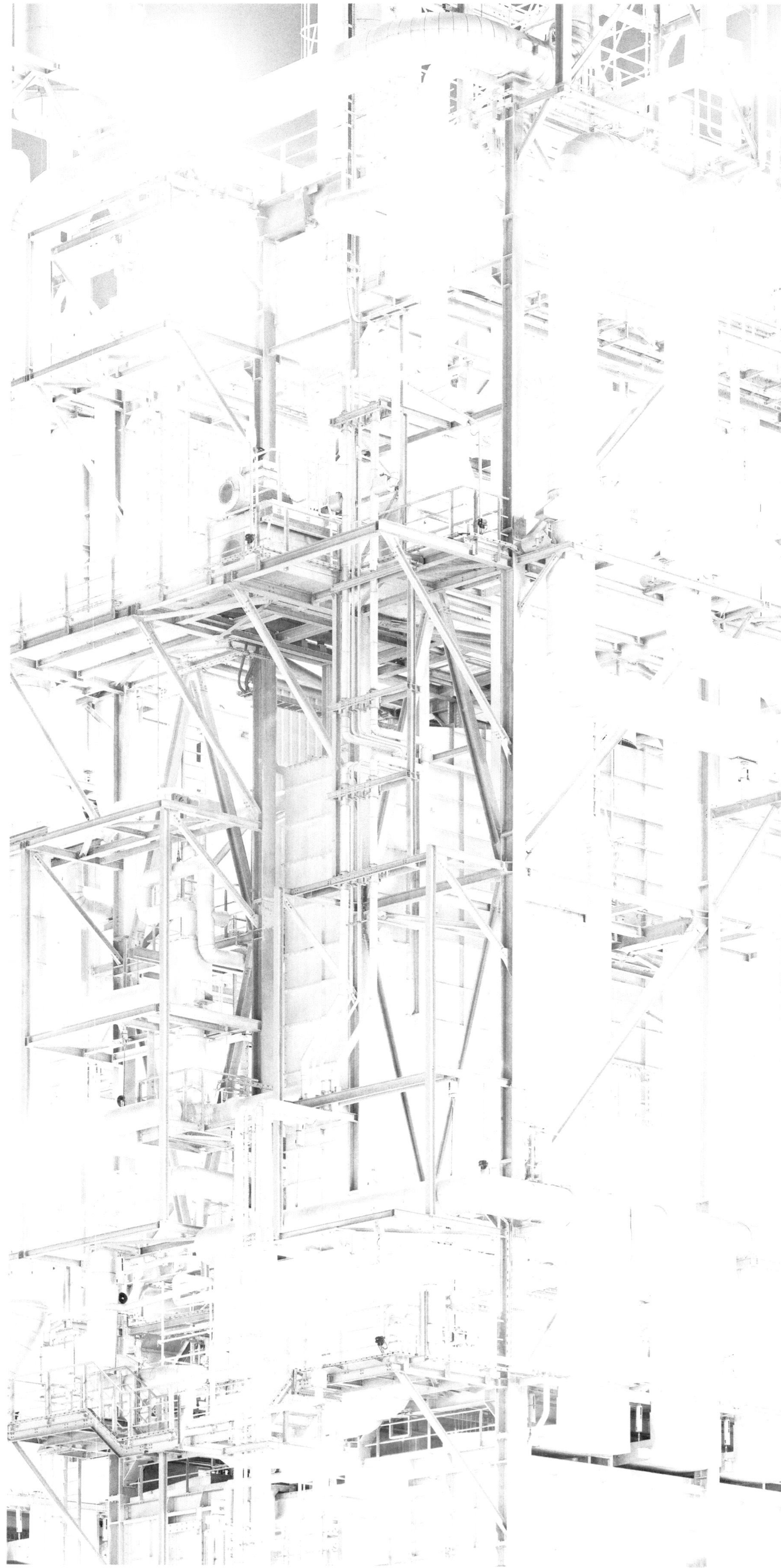

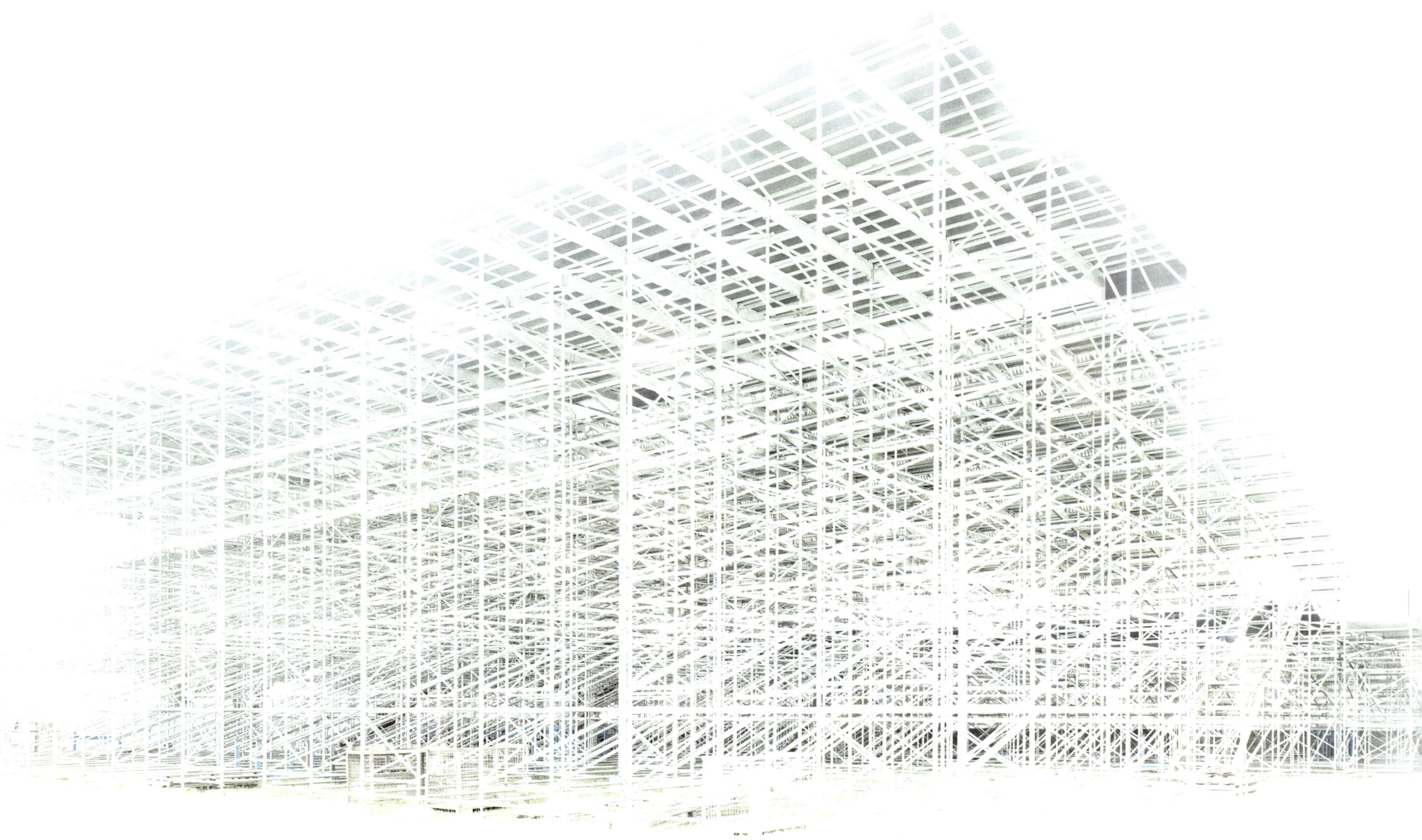

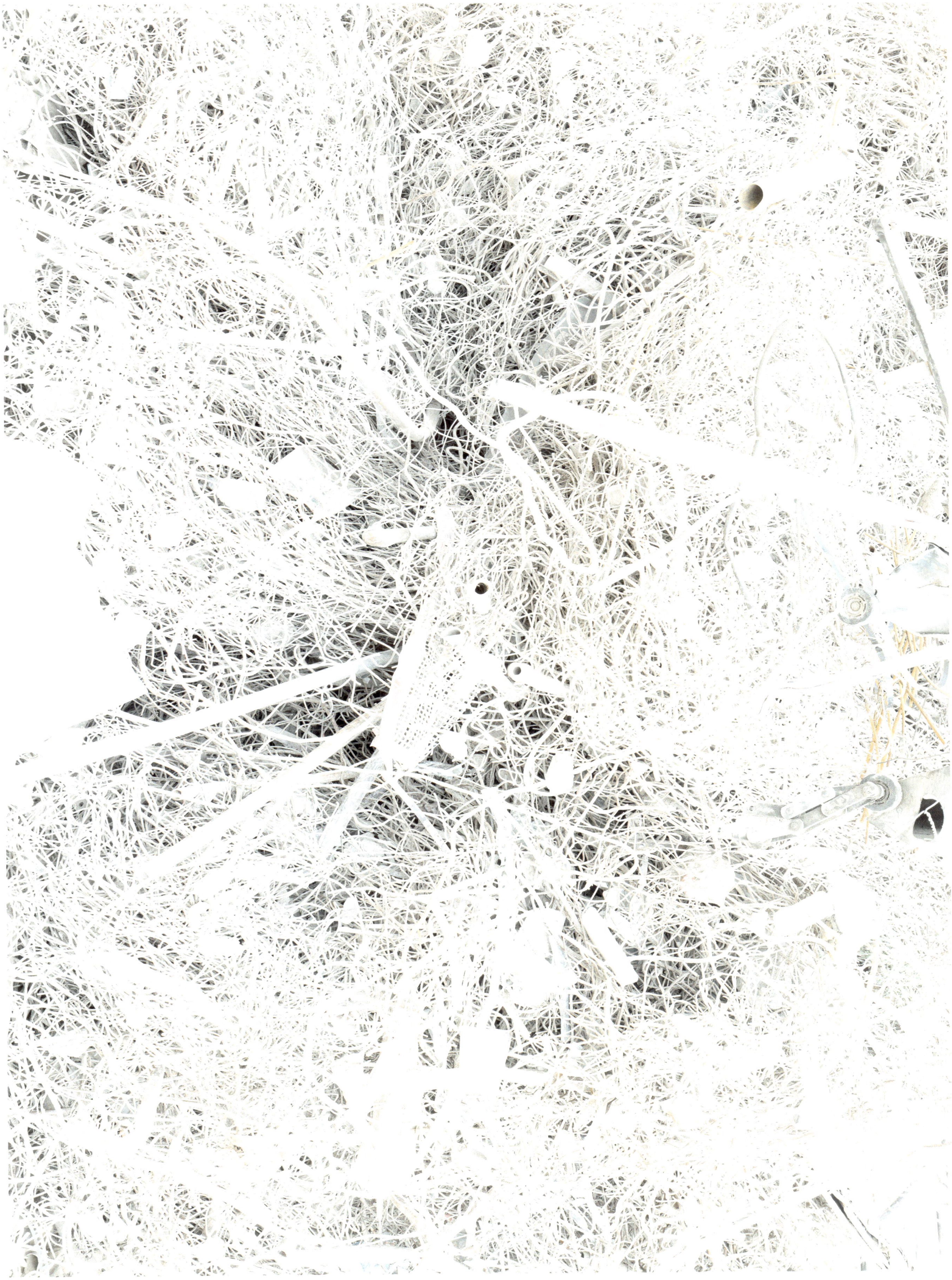

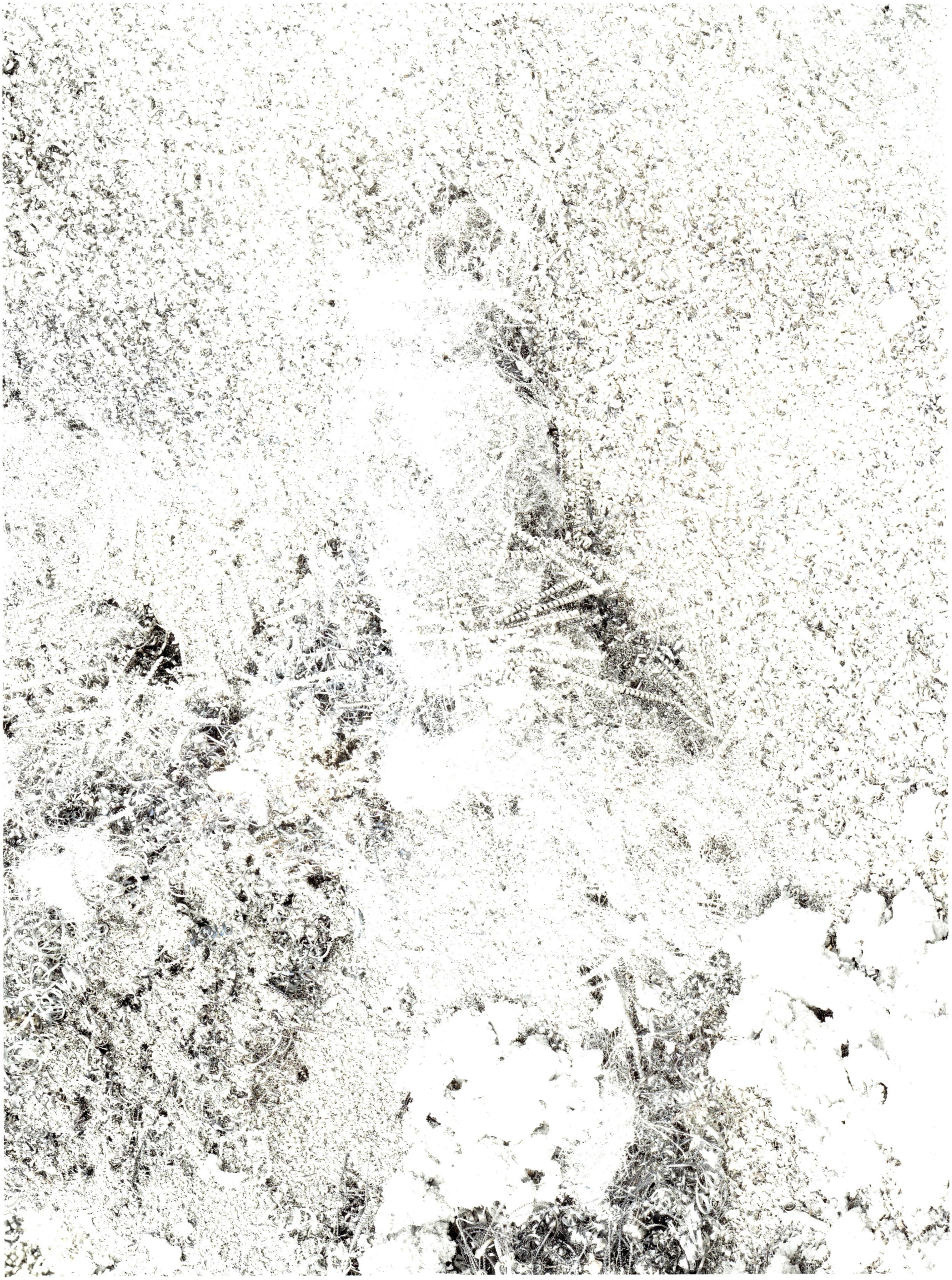

We are told we live in an age of enormous *visual appetites*. We run the risk of an *obesity of vision*, of swallowing more appearances than is good for us.

Instead, the real challenge we are faced with is the relation between appearance and meaning, appearance and revelation. Photography was a product of the industrial revolution

Paradoxically, this compu-terization, with its vast networks and easy replications, has produced its own enlargement and acceleration of our image culture.

What is vision for when the real forces that affect our lives have become invisible? Does the image world offer insight or distraction? Is vision being eclipsed?

We then ask the camera to spit out what it has swallowed onto a screen or onto paper. We must then re-swallow it with our own eyes.

We are told we live in an age of enormous *visual appetites*. We run the risk of an *obesity of vision*, of swallowing more appearances than is good for us.

culture, in which the eye is stimulated as never before. But visual stimulation is neither knowledge nor understanding, although it can play a part in both.

The anxiety that the world of images might disturb or distort civil society is familiar. How often do we hear that we are 'bombarded' or 'under siege' from pictures

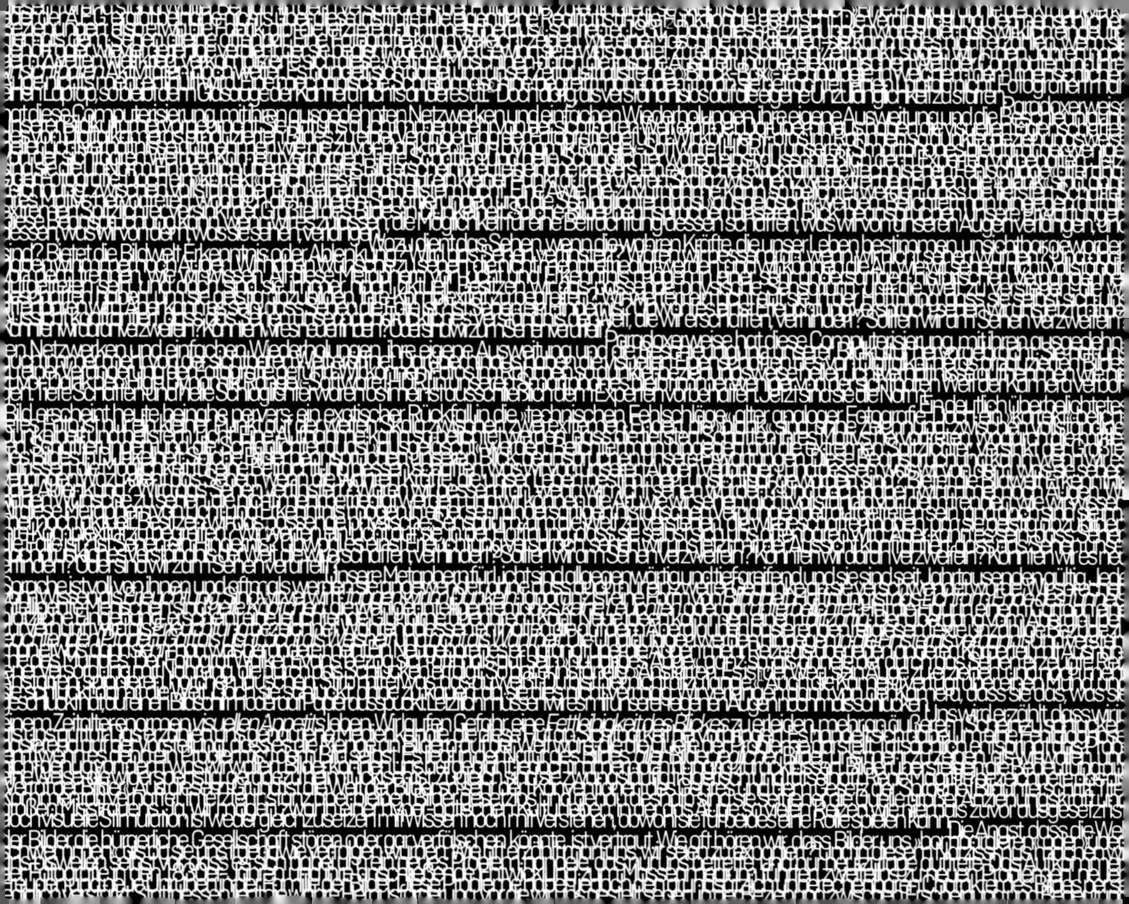

stimulated as never before. But visual stimulation is neither knowledge nor understanding, although it can play a part in both.

The anxiety that the world of images might disturb or distort civil society is familiar. How often do we hear that we are "bombarded" or "under siege" from pictures, as if somehow they were pursuing us? How often are we told we are *overexposed*? And in that narcissism we may delude ourselves that is a new problem, afflicting only us, and only now. The arrival of photography in the eighteen-thirties and its subsequent development into a mass medium certainly introduced new problems, new pleasures, and new disturbances into the family of images. But these have only exacerbated the essentially unpredictable condition of the image as such.

Instead, the real challenge we face has to do with the relation between appearance and meaning, or appearance and revelation. Photography was a product of the Industrial Revolution, and so it had a kinship with those industrial technologies that were discernible to the human eye, that could be understood visually. This was the world of pulleys and levers, of mechanical clocks and Aristotelian principles. One could look at a photograph of a steam engine and figure out how it worked. The relation between the mechanical world and photography was complementary. An optical-mechanical-chemical camera for a legible-mechanical-chemical world. Of course photography could not reveal the economics of mechanized industrialism, at least not in any immediate way. This is why Walter Benjamin was so suspicious of photography's promise of revelation. "A photograph of the Krupp works or the AEG tells us nothing about these institutions. Actual reality has slipped into the functional. The reification of human relations—the factory, say—means that they are no longer explicit," he wrote back in 1931.[2] But really those relations were never truly explicit, never fully revealed to vision alone. A photograph might be able to show how a machine works but it cannot tell you who owns it, or how much its operator is paid, or how much profit is generated.

At a later point, let's say in the years following the Second World War, that world of machines was complicated even further by the rapid spread of the electronic world of the computer and its *invisible* activities. This is our era of "black box" technology where nothing is revealed to the human eye. A mechanical typewriter can be understood by looking at it. Your laptop computer cannot. If you photograph your laptop the glass eye of your camera is left to stare blankly at its own inadequacy.

Paradoxically this computerization, with its vast networks and easy replications, has produced its own enlargement and acceleration of our image culture. Computerization has also offered ever more of the visible world to us. Moreover, the visual qualities of the image produced by digital cameras have transformed photography. We can take photographs in lower light and brighter light than ever before. The "high dynamic range" software in your

oder Erscheinung und Enthüllung. Die Fotografie war ein Produkt der industriellen Revolution und somit verwandt mit jenen industriellen Technologien, die für das menschliche Auge wahrnehmbar waren, die also visuell begriffen werden konnten. Das war die Welt der Flaschenzüge und Hebel, der mechanischen Uhren und aristotelischen Prinzipien. Man konnte die Fotografie einer Dampfmaschine betrachten und sich zusammenreimen, wie diese funktionierte. Die Beziehung zwischen mechanischer Welt und Fotografie war komplementär. Eine optisch-mechanisch-chemische Kamera für eine lesbare mechanisch-chemische Welt. Natürlich war die Fotografie nicht in der Lage, die Ökonomie des mechanisierten Industrialismus zu enthüllen, zumindest nicht auf eine unmittelbare Art und Weise. Aus diesem Grund stand Walter Benjamin dem Versprechen der Fotografie, zu enthüllen, so skeptisch gegenüber: »Eine Photographie der Kruppwerke oder der A.E.G. ergibt beinahe nichts über diese Institute. Die eigentliche Realität ist in die Funktionale gerutscht. Die Verdinglichung der menschlichen Beziehungen, also etwa die Fabrik, gibt die letzteren nicht mehr heraus«, schrieb er 1931.[2] Doch diese Beziehungen waren niemals wirklich eindeutig, niemals dem Sehen alleine offenbar. Eine Fotografie kann vielleicht zeigen, wie eine Maschine funktioniert, sie kann indes nicht erzählen, wem sie gehört oder wieviel derjenige verdient, der sie bedient, oder wieviel Gewinn sie erwirtschaftet.

Zu einem späteren Zeitpunkt, sagen wir, in den Jahren nach dem Zweiten Weltkrieg, verkomplizierte sich diese Welt der Maschinen durch die rasche Ausbreitung der elektronischen Welt der Computer und ihrer *unsichtbaren* Aktivitäten noch weiter. Es handelt sich dabei um unser Zeitalter der »Blackbox«-Technologie, in welchem dem menschlichen Auge nichts mehr enthüllt wird. Eine mechanische Schreibmaschine begreift man, indem man sie betrachtet. Einen Laptop nicht. Fotografiert man einen Laptop, so bleibt dem Glasauge der Kamera nichts anderes übrig, als verständnislos auf die eigene Unzulänglichkeit zu starren.

Paradoxerweise hat diese Computerisierung, mit ihren ausgedehnten Netzwerken und einfachen Wiederholungen, ihre eigene Ausweitung und die Beschleunigung unserer Bildkultur hervorgebracht. Sie hat uns auch immer mehr von der sichtbaren Welt eröffnet. Darüber hinaus haben die visuellen Eigenschaften des von Digitalkameras produzierten Bildes zu einer Veränderung der Fotografie geführt. Wir können Fotos im Rahmen so dunkler beziehungsweise heller Lichtverhältnisse aufnehmen wie nie zuvor. Dank der »High Dynamik Range«-Software (HDR) in unseren Smartphones bleibt immer weniger von der sichtbaren Welt der Kamera verborgen. Tiefe Schatten und helle Schlaglichter waren einst ausschließlich dem Experten vorbehalten. Jetzt sind sie die Norm.

Ein deutlich überbelichtetes Bild erscheint heute beinahe pervers, wie ein exotischer Rückfall in die »technischen Fehlschläge« alter analoger Fotografie. Doch ein »korrekt

smartphone means that less and less of the visible world escapes the camera. Deep shadows and bright highlights were once available only to the specialist. Now they are the norm.

A wildly overexposed image now seems almost perverse, an exotic throwback to the "technical failures" of old analog photography. But a "correctly" exposed photograph is a small point on the long scale between two blanks: complete darkness and complete light. A photograph can be made exposing for the deepest shadows of its subject, leaving the mid-tones and highlights to "blow out." Exposing for extreme highlights can plunge most of the image into blackness. Such images strain our sight, strain our expectations. This strain can, if we let it, open the possibility of a contemplation of just what it is we want from our eyes and what it is we want from what they see.

What is vision for when the real forces that affect our lives have become invisible? Does the image world offer insight or distraction? Is vision being eclipsed? Would we be better off not looking? And yet, we still have eyes. We have desires to look that cease to be satisfied and we cannot quite disentangle how we see from how we know. All those metaphors of light and knowledge may have appeared in a very different historical past but they are with us still. Do we have the right physical sensorium to understand the world we have made, to cognitively map it, to comprehend its complexity? We throw light at it, in the hope that it will reveal itself to us. But might it be that vision is the trap? Is vision an obstacle? While it once promised enlightenment are we now facing the prospect that vision is preventing our urgent comprehension of the world we are making? Should we give up on vision? Could we give up on it? Could we reinvent it? Or are we doomed to see?

belichtetes Foto ist nur ein kleiner Punkt auf der weiten Skala zwischen zwei extremen Enden, die »blank« sind, ohne Zeichnung: zwischen vollständiger Dunkelheit und hellstem Licht. Eine Aufnahme kann so belichtet werden, dass die tiefsten Schatten ihres Motivs hervortreten, wodurch die mittleren Schattierungen und die Schlaglichter quasi »ausgelöscht« werden. Belichtet man hingegen auf die extremen Spitzlichter, versinkt der Großteil des Bildes in Dunkelheit. Solche Bilder beanspruchen unseren Blick, beanspruchen unsere Erwartungen. Diese Beanspruchung kann, wenn wir es zulassen, die Möglichkeit für eine Betrachtung dessen schaffen, was wir von unseren Augen verlangen, und dessen, was wir von dem, was sie sehen, verlangen.

Wozu dient das Sehen, wenn die wahren Kräfte, die unser Leben bestimmen, unsichtbar geworden sind? Bietet die Bildwelt Erkenntnis oder Ablenkung? Wird das Sehen verfinstert? Wären wir besser dran, wenn wir nicht sehen würden? Und doch haben wir immer noch Augen. Wir haben Wünsche zu sehen, die nicht mehr befriedigt werden, und wir können die Art, wie wir sehen, nicht vollständig von dem trennen, wie wir wissen. All diese Metaphern von Licht und Erkenntnis mögen in einer sehr andersartigen historischen Vergangenheit aufgetreten sein, und doch sind sie immer noch aktuell. Besitzen wir das passende physische Sensorium, um die Welt zu verstehen, die wir geschaffen haben, um sie geistig abzubilden, ihre Komplexität zu begreifen? Wir werfen ein Licht auf sie, in der Hoffnung, dass sie selbst sich uns offenbaren wird. Aber kann es sein, dass Sehen die Falle ist? Ist Sehen ein Hindernis? Obwohl es einst Erleuchtung versprach, sehen wir uns jetzt mit der Aussicht konfrontiert, dass das Sehen unser nachdrückliches Verständnis der Welt, die wir erschaffen, verhindert? Sollten wir am Sehen verzweifeln? Könnten wir daran verzweifeln? Könnten wir es neu erfinden? Oder sind wir zum Sehen verurteilt?

[1] Walker Evans as quoted in *Walker Evans: Many Are Called,* ed. Jeff Rosenhein (New Haven, CT, 2004), p. 208.

[2] Walter Benjamin, "A Short History of Photography" (1931), in *One-Way Street and Other Writings,* trans. J. A. Underwood (London, 1978), pp. 240–257.

[1] Zit. n. Roswell Angier, *Schärfe deinen Blick. Außergewöhnliche Portraitfotografie in Kontext, Theorie und Praxis,* München 2007, S. 61.

[2] Walter Benjamin, »Kleine Geschichte der Photographie«, in: ders., *Das Kunstwerk im Zeitalter seiner technischen Reproduzierbarkeit. Drei Studien zur Kunstsoziologie* (edition suhrkamp, 28), Frankfurt am Main 1977, S. 45–64, hier S. 63 (nach Brecht).

APPENDIX

THE WORKS DIE ARBEITEN

The photographs in the *Blank* series were taken primarily at night and without the use of additional artificial light. Using long exposures and multiple shots in a complex process results in extremely bright images with completely empty—blank—areas and in some, areas with the finest details. The resemblance to drawings or the impression of photographic negatives is the result of the extreme overexposure, while the digital post-production is mainly limited to assembling the individual photographs. Unlike the others, the photographs with the designation *SV,* were taken by *ISS* crew members and are the original material, which has subsequently been markedly processed on the computer, for example, through the repositioning of details as well as strong contrast and changes in color.
All works are inkjet prints on fine art paper, ash frames, which are either black or white, and museum quality glass. The dimensions given refer to the image size. *SV 01–SV 21:* frame size plus approximately 3 cm. All other works: frame size plus approximately 7 cm.

Die Fotografien der Serie *Blank* werden überwiegend nachts ohne Verwendung zusätzlichen künstlichen Lichts aufgenommen. Mithilfe von Langzeitbelichtungen und Mehrfachaufnahmen entstehen in einer aufwendigen Technik extrem helle Bilder mit komplett leeren – blanken – Bereichen und anderen mit feinsten Details. Der an Zeichnungen oder fotografische Negative erinnernde Eindruck ist einzig ein Resultat der extremen Überbelichtung, während sich die digitale Postproduktion im Wesentlichen auf das Zusammensetzen der Einzelaufnahmen beschränkt. Anders bei den Bildern mit der Bezeichnung *SV:* Fotos, die von der Besatzung der ISS gemacht wurden, sind hier das Ursprungsmaterial, das am Computer deutlich bearbeitet wird, beispielsweise durch das Umsetzen von Details sowie starken Kontrast- und Farbänderungen.
Alle Arbeiten sind Inkjetprints auf Fine-Art-Papier, mit schwarz oder weiß lackierten Holzrahmen (Esche) und hinter Museumsglas. Die Größenangaben beziehen sich auf die Bildgröße. *SV 01–SV 21:* Rahmenaußenmaß plus ca. 3 cm. Alle anderen Arbeiten: Rahmenaußenmaß plus ca. 7 cm.

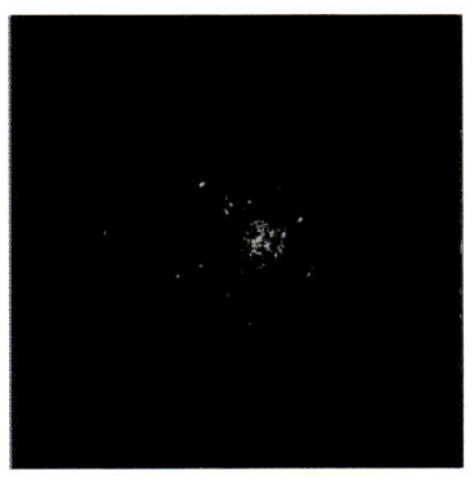

SV 15
Gulf of Tonkin Golf von Tonkin 2015
12.6 x 12.6 in. 32 x 32 cm

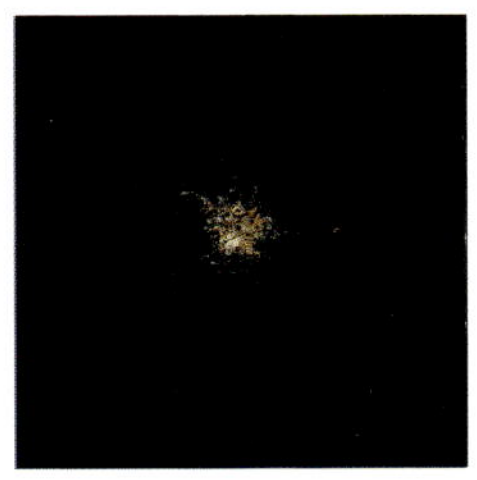

SV 20
Salerno 2015
12.6 x 12.6 in. 32 x 32 cm

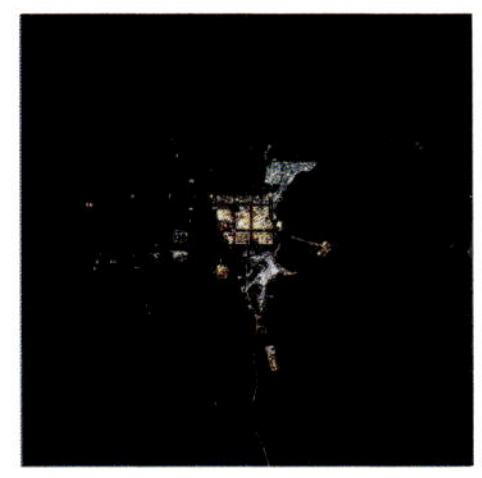

SV 07
Jubail 2012
12.6 x 12.6 in. 32 x 32 cm

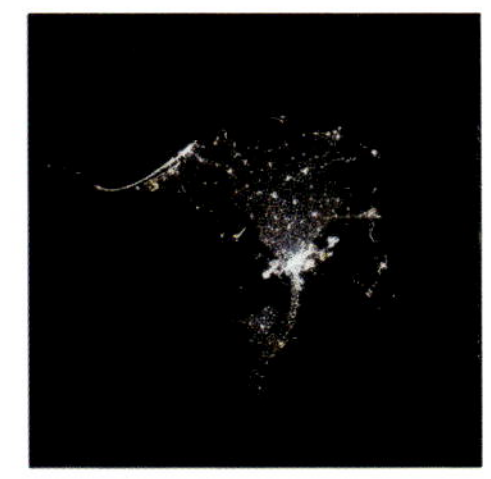

SV 11
Cairo Kairo 2015
12.6 x 12.6 in. 32 x 32 cm

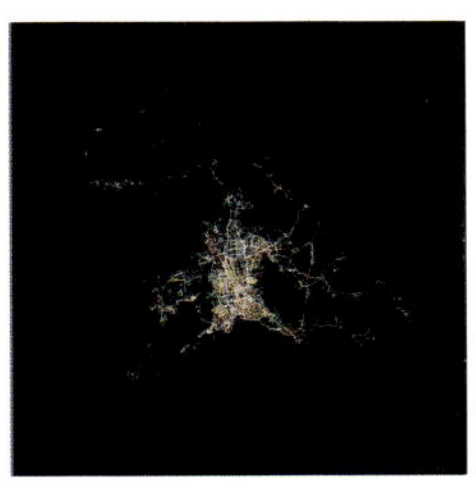

SV 12
Athens Athen 2015
12.6 x 12.6 in. 32 x 32 cm

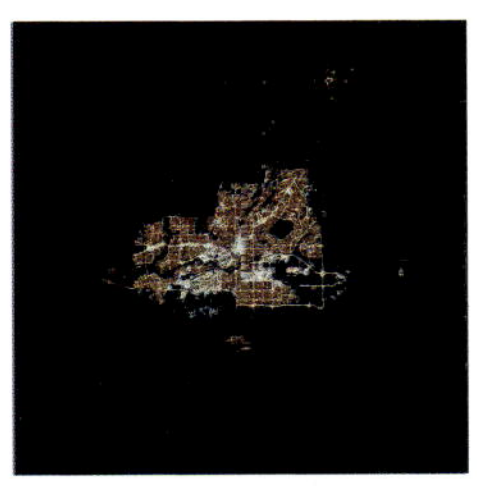

SV 05
Calgary 2012
12.6 x 12.6 in. 32 x 32 cm

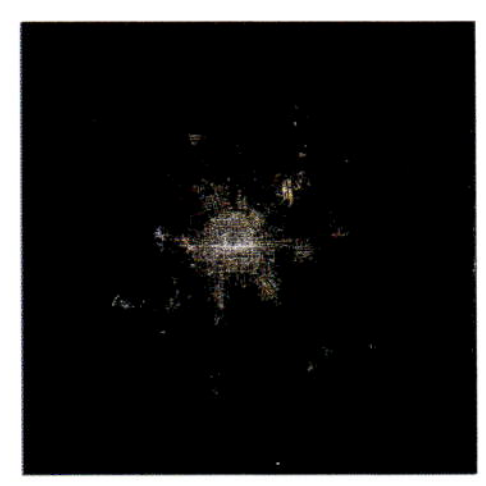

SV 06
Beijing Peking 2012
12.6 x 12.6 in. 32 x 32 cm

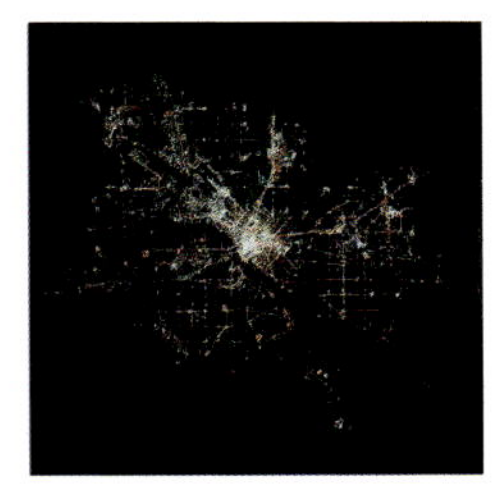

SV 08
Dallas 2012
12.6 x 12.6 in. 32 x 32 cm

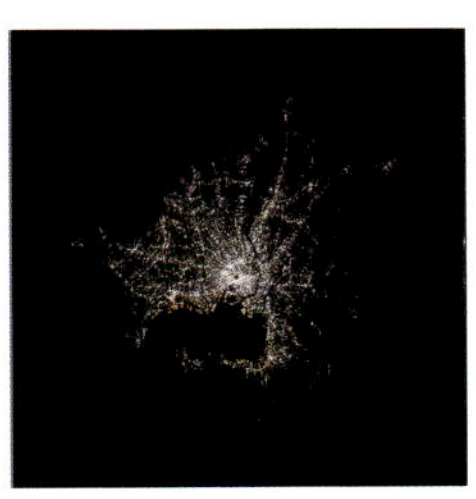

SV 14
Tokyo Tokio 2015
12.6 x 12.6 in. 32 x 32 cm

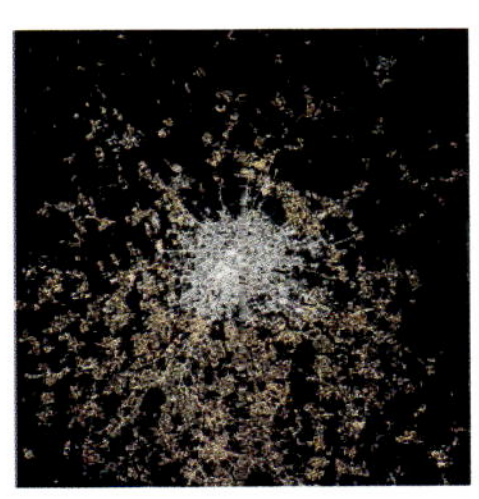

SV 21
Milan Mailand 2015
12.6 x 12.6 in. 32 x 32 cm

CS 14
Tokyo Tokio 2010
46.1 x 95.7 in. 117 x 243 cm

CS 20
Seoul 2014
46.1 x 76.0 in. 117 x 193 cm

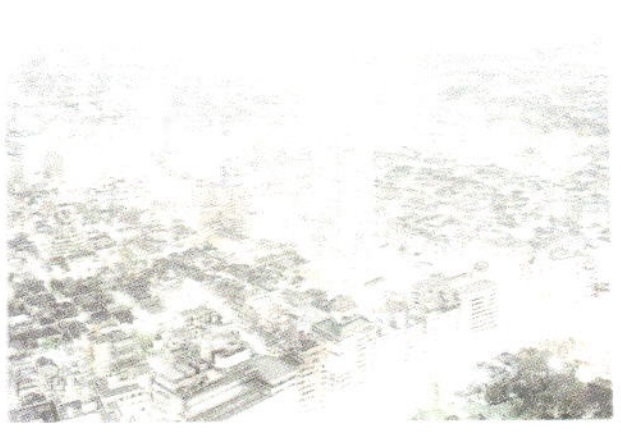

CS 02
Tokyo Tokio 2010
59.1 x 78.7 in. 150 x 200 cm

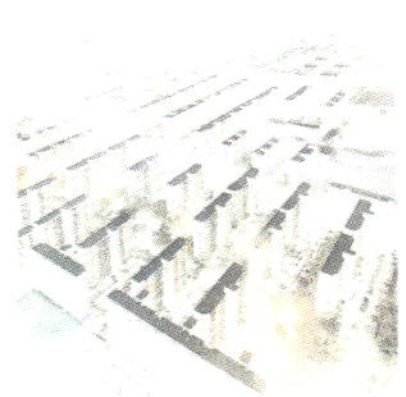

CS 17
Seoul 2014
46.1 x 36.2 in. 117 x 92 cm

CS 16
Seoul 2014
46.1 x 74.8 in. 117 x 190 cm

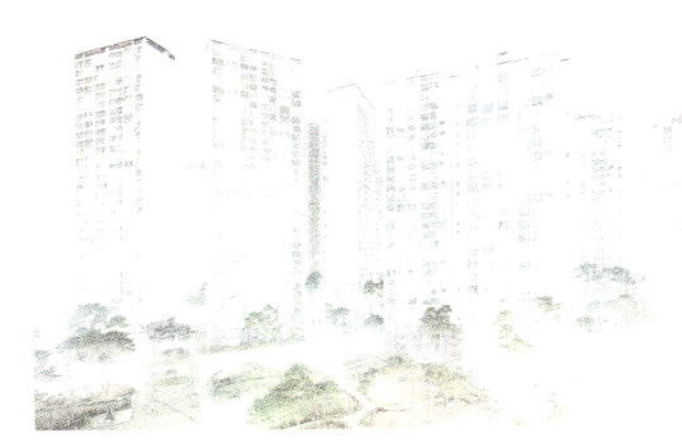

CS 19
Seoul 2014
46.1 x 63.4 in. 117 x 161 cm

FR 01
Tokyo Tokio 2010
46.1 x 53.5 in. 117 x 136 cm

FR 31
Seoul 2014
59.1 x 52.4 in. 150 x 133 cm

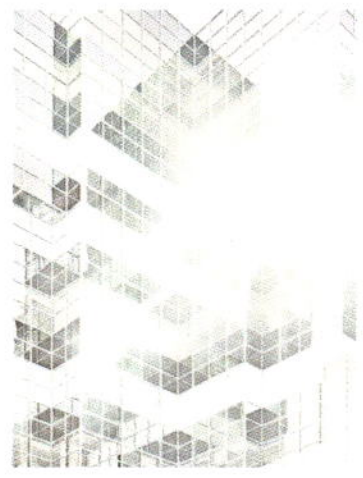

FR 11
London 2012
37.4 x 28.3 in. 95 x 72 cm

FR 17
Rotterdam 2013
59.1 x 43.3 in. 150 x 110 cm

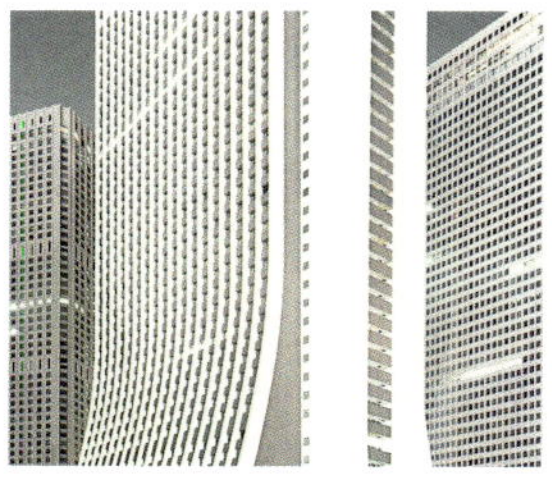

FR 07
Tokyo Tokio 2010
46.1 x 54.3 in. 117 x 138 cm

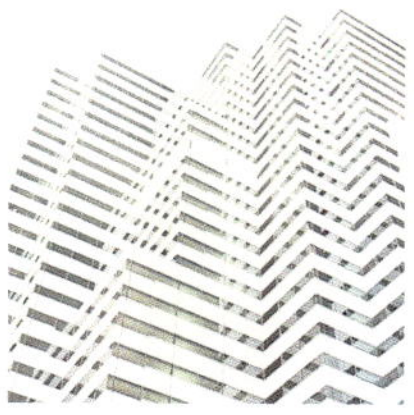

FR 06
Tokyo Tokio 2012
37.4 x 32.7 in. 95 x 83 cm

FR 25
Seoul 2014
46.1 x 35.0 in. 117 x 89 cm

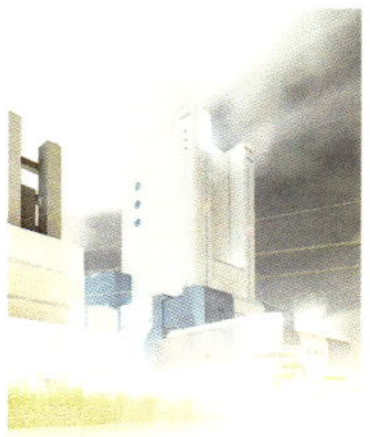

IP 19
Bergheim 2014
46.1 x 35.8 in. 117 x 91 cm

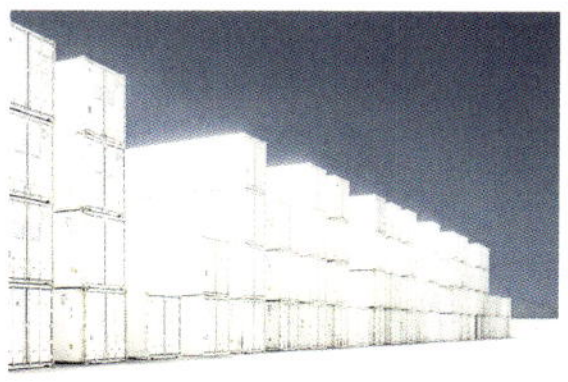

IP 11
Bremerhaven 2012
46.1 x 55.9 in. 117 x 142 cm

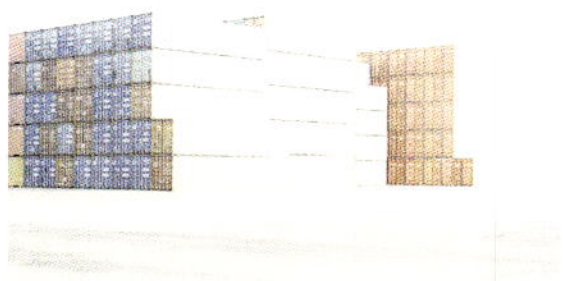

IP 02
Osaka 2011
29.5 x 36.2 in. 75 x 92 cm

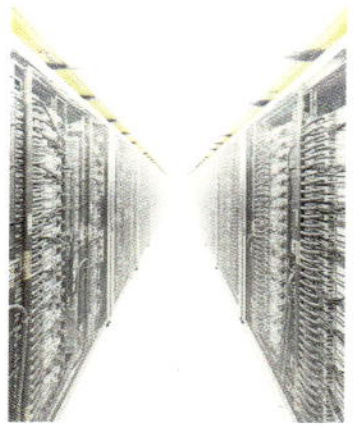

IP 32
Garching 2014
46.1 x 34.2 in. 117 x 87 cm

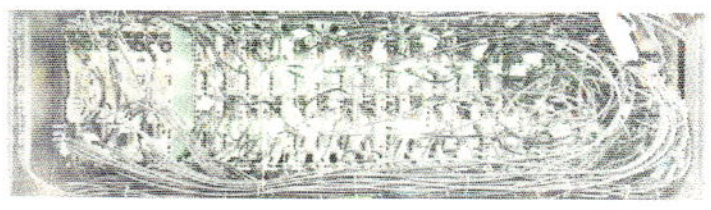

IP 33
Garching 2014
29.5 x 81.5 in. 75 x 207 cm

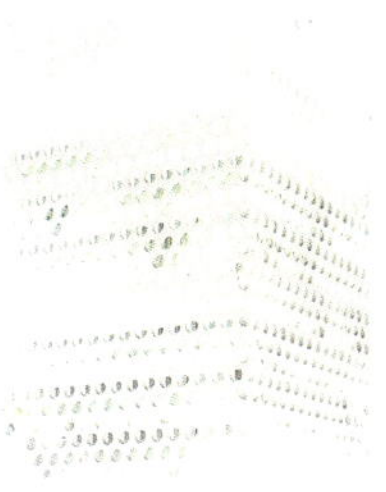

FR 27
Seoul 2014
37.4 x 30.3 in. 95 x 77 cm

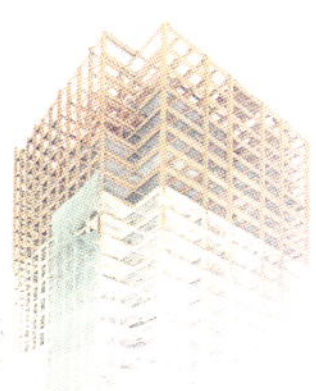

FR 26
Seoul 2014
46.1 x 38.6 in. 117 x 98 cm

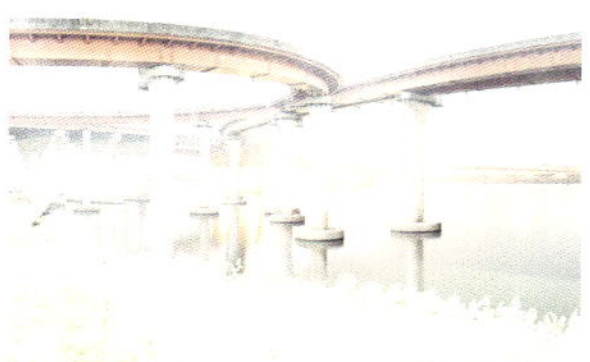

CS 15
Seoul 2014
46.1 x 58.3 in. 117 x 148 cm

CS 12
Osaka 2011
46.1 x 54.3 in. 117 x 138 cm

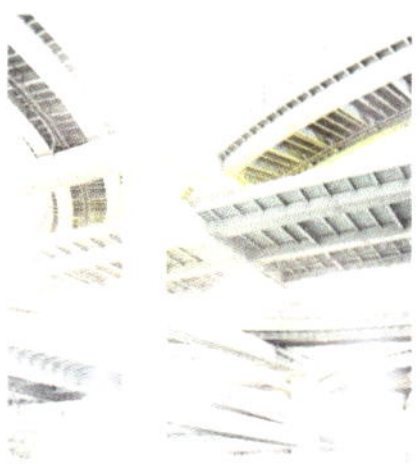

CS 13
Osaka 2011
63.0 x 58.7 in. 160 x 149 cm

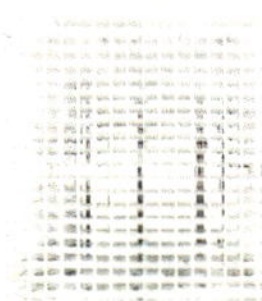

FR 22
Brussels Brüssel 2014
59.1 x 49.6 in. 150 x 126 cm

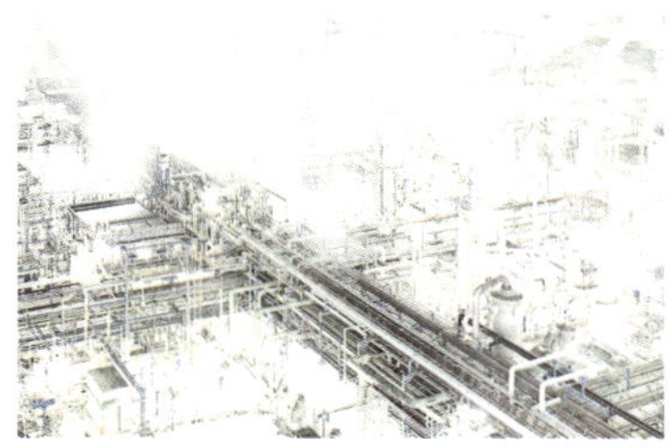

IP 13
Gelsenkirchen 2012
46.1 x 70.9 in. 117 x 180 cm

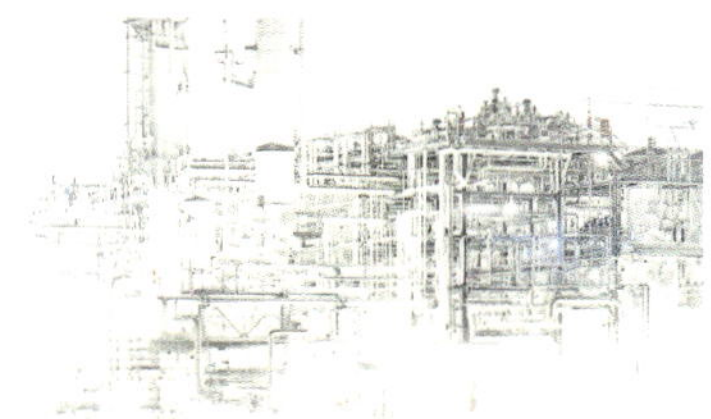

IP 12
Dormagen 2012
46.1 x 68.5 in. 117 x 174 cm

IP 06
Osaka 2011
46.1 x 66.1 in. 117 x 168 cm

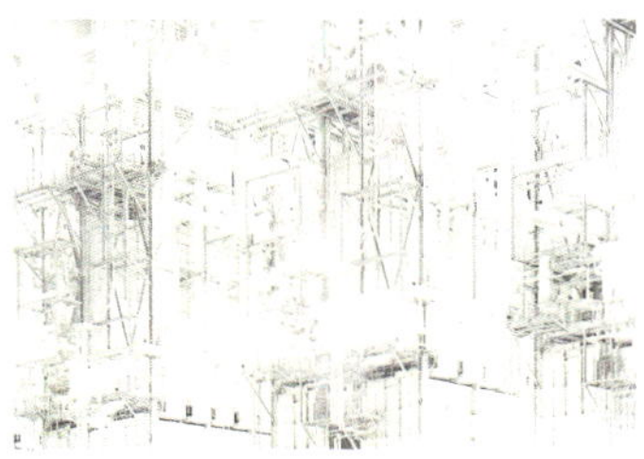

IP 15
Gelsenkirchen 2012
46.1 x 66.9 in. 117 x 170 cm

IP 16
Düsseldorf 2014
37.4 x 51.2 in. 95 x 130 cm

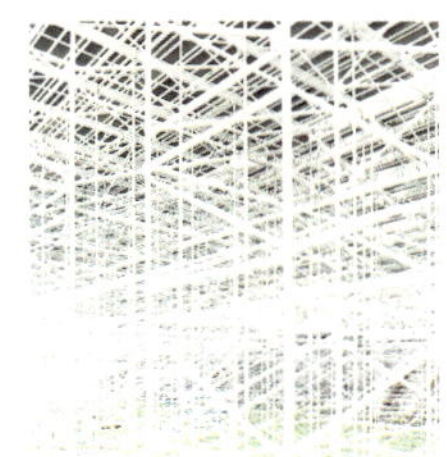

IP 18
Düsseldorf 2014
59.1 x 53.5 in. 150 x 136 cm

IP 22
Neuss 2014
59.1 x 53.5 in. 150 x 136 cm

IP 23
Neuss 2014
59.1 x 53.9 in. 150 x 137 cm

IP 21
Neuss 2014
46.1 x 59.1 in. 117 x 150 cm

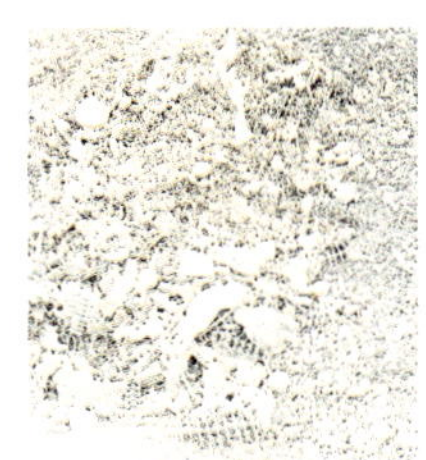

IP 37
Neuss 2014
46.1 x 39.4 in. 117 x 100 cm

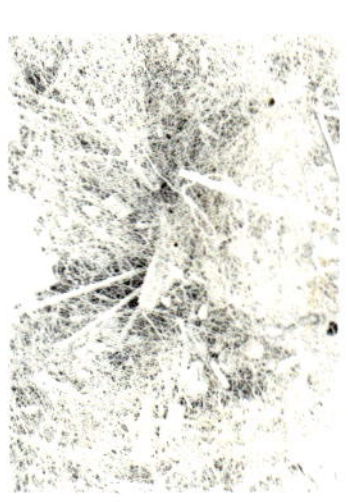

IP 20
Neuss 2014
46.1 x 33.5 in. 117 x 85 cm

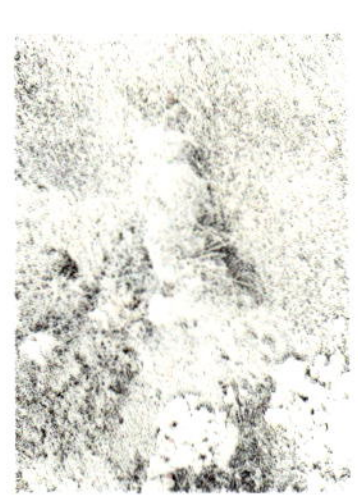

IP 25
Neuss 2014
46.1 x 33.9 in. 117 x 86 cm

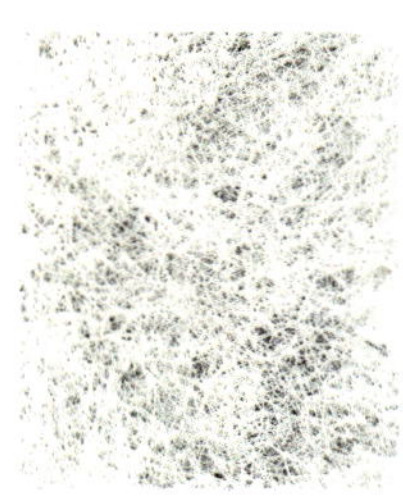

IP 41
Folegandros 2015
29.5 x 24.3 in. 75 x 63 cm

ANDREAS GEFELLER

Andreas Gefeller (*1970) studied photography at the University of Essen and completed his degree with honors under Bernhard Prinz in 2000. Gefeller was appointed to the Deutsche Fotografische Akademie in 2001. He lives and works in Düsseldorf.

Andreas Gefeller (*1970) studierte an der Universität Essen Fotografie und schloss 2000 sein Studium bei Bernhard Prinz mit Auszeichnung ab. Gefeller, der 2001 in die Deutsche Fotografische Akademie berufen wurde, lebt und arbeitet in Düsseldorf.

SOLO EXHIBITIONS EINZELAUSSTELLUNGEN

2016 *Andreas Gefeller,* Thomas Rehbein Galerie, Cologne Köln
2015 *Andreas Gefeller,* Dear Future Me, Brussels Brüssel
2014 *Andreas Gefeller—Fotografien 2000–2014,* Palais für aktuelle Kunst, Glückstadt
Supervisions and Beyond, Baton Gallery, Seoul
2012 *Blank,* Thomas Rehbein Galerie, Cologne Köln
2011 *The Japan Series,* Hasted Kraeutler, New York
Photographs, Kunsthalle Erfurt, Erfurt
2010 *The Japan Series,* Thomas Rehbein Galerie, Cologne Köln
Photographs, Landesgalerie Linz, Linz
Photographs, Münchner Stadtmuseum, Sammlung Fotografie, Munich München
2009 *Photographs,* Stadtgalerie, Saarbrücken
New Works, Hasted Hunt, New York
2008 *Supervisions,* Kunstverein Augsburg, Augsburg
Andreas Gefeller, Thomas Rehbein Galerie, Cologne Köln
2007 *Supervisions,* Hasted Hunt, New York
Supervisions, Kunstverein Heinsberg, Heinsberg
2006 *Supernatural,* Dubbelbee Gallery, Amsterdam
2005 *Supervisions,* BAT CampusGalerie, Bayreuth
2004 *Kunstpreis der Stadt Nordhorn,* Städtische Galerie Nordhorn, Nordhorn
Supervisions, Thomas Rehbein Galerie, Cologne Köln

GROUP EXHIBITIONS GRUPPENAUSSTELLUNGEN

2016 *Up / Down,* Holden Gallery, Manchester
Momente der Auflösung, Marta Herford, Herford
2015 *Ein Moment: Ewig,* Kunstwerk—Sammlung Alison und Peter W. Klein, Nussdorf
Small Worlds, The New Art Gallery Walsall, Walsall
Über Wasser, Bucerius Kunst Forum, Hamburg
Photo Beijing 2015, China Millennium Monument, Beijing Peking
Highlights, Thomas Rehbein Galerie, Cologne Köln
Macht und Gewalt—Ohnmacht und Widerstand, Neuer Kunstverein Aschaffenburg e.V., Aschaffenburg
2014 *Celebrated,* Atlas Gallery, London
Trace 14, Elgiz Museum, Istanbul
Landschaft im Dekolleté, Opelvillen Rüsselsheim, Rüsselsheim
One Million Traces, Kunstverein Duisburg, Duisburg
Heimat, NRW-Forum, Düsseldorf
2013 *Lead Awards,* Haus der Photographie, Hamburg
An Idea of Beauty, Palazzo Strozzi, Florence Florenz

Metropolis: Reflections on the Modern City, Birmingham Museum and Art Gallery, Birmingham
Farbe Form Fotografie Fläche, Art Foyer DZ Bank, Frankfurt am Main
Vues d'en haut, Centre Pompidou Metz, Metz
Light Sensitive, The Nasher Museum of Art at Duke University, Durham, North Carolina

2012 *Wasserstandsmeldung*, Kunstmuseum Bonn, Bonn
Religion & Riten, Art Foyer DZ Bank, Frankfurt am Main
Points of View, Roemer- und Pelizaeus-Museum, Hildesheim
Lead Awards, Haus der Photographie, Hamburg
Out of Focus, Saatchi Gallery, London
Obsessions, La Filature, Mulhouse Mühlhausen, France Frankreich
Dark Sights, Art Foyer DZ Bank, Frankfurt am Main

2011 *The Detour of the Real*, Seoul Photography Festival, Seoul Museum of Art, Seoul
European Eyes on Japan / Japan Today Vol. 12, Prefectural Museum, Tottori
Noorderlicht Photofestival, Groningen
Spektrale 2011, Rheingoldhalle, Mainz
Für Hund und Katz ist auch noch Platz, Art Foyer DZ Bank, Frankfurt am Main
Size Matters: Large Scale European Photography, art: sensus, London
A to Z: 26 Great Photographs from the Norton Collection, Norton Museum of Art, West Palm Beach, Florida
Spannungsbogen: Figur und Raum, Kunstmuseum Dieselkraftwerk, Cottbus
Alison + Peter Klein Photo Art Award, Kunstwerk, Nussdorf

2010 *European Eyes on Japan / Japan Today Vol. 12*, Antrepo No. 5, Istanbul
Landscape without Horizon *Landschaft ohne Horizont*, Museum Schloss Moyland, Bedburg-Hau

2009 *Pittoresk: Neue Perspektiven auf das Landschaftsbild*, Marta Herford, Herford
Realtà Manipolate / Manipulating Reality, Palazzo Strozzi, Florence Florenz
Ferne Nähe, Kunstmuseum Bonn, Bonn
Veto—Zeitgenössische Positionen in der deutschen Fotografie, Haus der Photographie, Hamburg
Nature and Nation, Museum on the Seam, Jerusalem

2008 *Wert-Schätzung*, Sander Collection, Berlin
Rethinking Landscape, Taubman Museum of Art, Roanoke, Virginia
Human / Nature, Nelson-Atkins Museum of Art, Kansas City, Missouri
Support the Bauhaus!, Bauhaus-Archiv, Berlin
Chisel, New York Photography Festival, New York
Angelandet, Kunstmuseum Dieselkraftwerk, Cottbus

2007 *Made in Germany*, Kunstverein Hannover, Hannover
Spectacular City, NRW-Forum, Düsseldorf
Unter Sternen—Aus der Sammlung Willy Michel, Museum Franz Gertsch, Burgdorf

2006 *Tschernobyl*, Willy-Brandt-Haus, Berlin
Perceptions of Everyday Life, Veletrzni Palace, Prague Prag
Room with a View, Gemeentemuseum Den Haag, The Hague Den Haag
Prix du Festival Voies Off, Arles
Homestories, Galerie Münsterland, Emsdetten
Spectacular City, Netherlands Architecture Institute, Rotterdam

2005 *Les Grands Spectacles*, Museum der Moderne, Salzburg
Open ev+a, Limerick City Gallery of Art, Limerick

2004 *Gezähmte Natur*, Brandenburgische Kunstsammlungen, Cottbus
Urbane Räume, Goethe-Institut, Budapest
Biennale de Liège, Espace d'Art Contemporain, Liège Lüttich

2003 *Große Kunstausstellung NRW*, Museum Kunstpalast, Düsseldorf
Noorderlicht Photofestival, Groningen
Rückblende: Hochsommer, Kunsthaus Kaufbeuren, Kaufbeuren
Urbane Räume, Kunst- und Ausstellungshalle der Bundesrepublik Deutschland, Bonn

2002 *Peter Keetman Prize* *Peter-Keetman-Preis*, Museum der Arbeit, Hamburg

2001 *Reinhart Wolf Award* *Reinhart-Wolf-Preis*, Museum für Kunst und Gewerbe, Hamburg

CATALOGUES KATALOGE

Museum Unplugged: Eine Selbstbefragung. Edited by Hrsg. von Friedrich von Borries and und Roland Nachtigäller. Exh. cat. Ausst.-Kat. Marta Herford, Herford. Altenburg, 2015.

Art from Elsewhere. Edited by Hrsg. von David Elliot. Exh. cat. Ausst.-Kat. Hayward Gallery, London. London, 2014.

Ewing, William A. *Landmark: The Fields of Landscape Photography*. London, 2014.

Feireiss, Lukas, and und Robert Klanten. *Imagine Architecture: Artistic Visions of the Urban Realm*. Berlin, 2014.

An Idea of Beauty. Edited by Hrsg. von Franziska Nori. Exh. cat. Ausst.-Kat. Palazzo Strozzi, Florence Florenz. Florence Florenz, 2013.

Heimat—No Place Like Home. Edited by Hrsg. von Hans Georg Näder and und Sebastian Peichl. Exh. cat. Ausst.-Kat. Kunsthalle HGN, Duderstadt. Duderstadt, 2013.

Higgins, Jackie. *Why It Does Not Have to Be in Focus: Modern Photography Explained*. London, 2013.

Vues d'en haut. Edited by Hrsg. von Angela Lampe. Exh. cat. Ausst.-Kat. Centre Pompidou Metz. Metz, 2013.

Corporate Collections. Edited by Hrsg. von Friedrich Georg Conzen and und Olaf Salié. Cologne Köln, 2012.

Klein, Kelly. *Pools: Reflections*. New York, 2012.

Out of Focus: Photography. Edited by Hrsg. von William A. Ewing. Exh. cat. Ausst.-Kat. Saatchi Gallery, London. London, 2012.

Points of View: Orte der Fotografie. Edited by Hrsg. von Torsten Scheid. Exh. cat. Ausst.-Kat. Roemer- und Pelizaeus-Museum, Hildesheim. Heidelberg, 2012.

Power: Prix Pictet 04. Exh. cat. Ausst.-Kat. Prix Pictet. Kempen, 2012.

Metropolis. Exh. cat. Ausst.-Kat. Noorderlicht Photography Foundation, Groningen. Amsterdam, 2011.

New York: A Photographer's City. Edited by Hrsg. von Marla Hamburg Kennedy. New York, 2011.

Veto—Zeitgenössische Positionen in der deutschen Fotografie. Edited by Hrsg. von Ingo Taubhorn. Haus der Photographie, Hamburg. Heidelberg, 2011.

European Eyes on Japan / Japan Today Vol. 12. Exh. cat. Ausst.-Kat. EU-Japan Fest. Tokyo Tokio, 2010.

Landscape without Horizon / Landschaft ohne Horizont. Edited by Hrsg. von Bettina Paust. Exh. cat. Ausst.-Kat. Museum Schloss Moyland, Betburg-Hau. Nuremberg Nürnberg, 2010.

Beyond Architecture: Imaginative Buildings and Fictional Buildings. Edited by Hrsg. von Lukas Feireiss and und Robert Klanten. Berlin, 2009.

Ferne Nähe: Natur in der Kunst der Gegenwart. Edited by Hrsg. von Volker Adolphs, Stephan Berg, and und Martin Seel. Exh. cat. Ausst.-Kat. Kunstmuseum Bonn, Bonn. Cologne Köln, 2009.

Nature and Nation. Exh. cat. Ausst.-Kat. Museum on the Seam, Jerusalem. Jerusalem, 2009.

Photography Discussed: Images from the Tosca Photography Fund. Edited by Hrsg. von Simon Baker and und David Campany, et. al. u. a. London, 2009.

Pittoresk: Neue Perspektiven auf das Landschaftsbild. Edited by Hrsg. von Roland Nachtigäller and und Philippe Van Cauteren. Exh. cat. Ausst.-Kat. Marta Herford, Herford. Bramsche, 2009.

Realtà Manipolate. Exh. cat. Ausst.-Kat. Palazzo Strozzi, Florence Florenz. Florence Florenz, 2009.

Wert-Schätzung. Edited by Hrsg. von Anna-Catharina Gebbers. Nuremberg Nürnberg, 2008.

Made in Germany. Edited by Hrsg. von Andrea Gothe. Heidelberg, 2008.

Real Photography Award. Edited by Hrsg. von ING Real Estate. Exh. cat. Ausst.-Kat. LP2, Rotterdam. Zutphen, 2008.

Rethinking Landscape: Photographs from the Collection of Allen G. Thomas, Jr. Edited by Hrsg. von David J. Brown and und Dennis P. Weller. Exh. cat. Ausst.-Kat. Taubman Museum of Art, Roanoke. Roanoke, Virginia, 2008.

Made in Germany: Aktuelle Kunst aus Deutschland / Young Contemporary Art from Germany. Edited by Hrsg. von Martin Engler. Exh. cat. Ausst.-Kat. Kestnergesellschaft Hannover and und Sprengel Museum Hannover. Ostfildern, 2007.

Überblick: Konstruktionen der Wahrheit. Edited by Hrsg. von Albrecht Haag and und Alexandra Lechner. Exh. cat. Ausst.-Kat. Darmstädter Tage der Fotografie. Darmstadt, 2007.

Unter Sternen—Aus der Sammlung Willy Michel. Edited by Hrsg. von Katharina Pilz. Exh. cat. Ausst.-Kat. Museum Franz Gertsch, Burgdorf. Burgdorf, 2007.

Spectacular City: Photographing the Future. Edited by Hrsg. von Emiliano Gandolfi. Exh. cat. Ausst.-Kat. Netherlands Architecture Institute, Rotterdam. Rotterdam, 2006.

Hidden Sites. Edited by Hrsg. von Noorderlicht Photography Foundation, Groningen. Groningen, 2005.

Les Grands Spectacles: 120 Jahre Kunst und Massenkultur. Edited by Hrsg. von Agnes Husslein-Arco. Exh. cat. Ausst.-Kat. Museum der Moderne, Salzburg. Salzburg, 2005.

Open eva. Exh. cat. Ausst.-Kat. Limerick City Gallery of Art, Limerick. Oysterhaven, 2005.

Gezähmte Natur. Edited by Hrsg. von Verein der Freunde der Brandenburgischen Kunstsammlungen Cottbus and und Carmen Schliebe. Exh. cat. Ausst.-Kat. Brandenburgische Kunstsammlungen Cottbus. Cottbus, 2004.

Metamorfoses do Real—Encontros da Imagem. Edited by Hrsg. von Rui Prata. Braga, 2004.

Global Detail. Exh. cat. Ausst.-Kat. Noorderlicht Photography Foundation, Groningen. Groningen, 2003.

Rückblende: Hochsommer. Gemälde, Fotografie, Experimente. Edited by Hrsg. von Ulrich Heiß and und Anne-Cécile Foulon. Exh. cat. Ausst.-Kat. Kunsthaus Kaufbeuren. Kaufbeuren, 2003.

Industriefotografie. Edited by Hrsg. von Volkswagen Art Foundation. Heidelberg, 2002.

MONOGRAPHS MONOGRAFIEN

Blank. Ostfildern, 2016.

The Japan Series. Ostfildern, 2011.

Photographs. Edited by Hrsg. von Ernest W. Uthemann. Exh. cat. Ausst.-Kat. Stadtgalerie Saarbrücken. Ostfildern, 2009.

Andreas Gefeller. British American Tobacco. Bayreuth, 2005.

Supervisions. Edited by Hrsg. von Roland Nachtigäller. Exh. cat. Ausst.-Kat. Städtische Galerie Nordhorn. Ostfildern, 2005.

Soma. Ostfildern, 2003.

AWARDS AUSZEICHNUNGEN

2013 Lead Awards, Hamburg: Silver Silber
2012 Lead Awards, Hamburg: Honorable Mention Auszeichnung
Prix Pictet, London: Nominee Nominierung
Deutsche Börse Photography Prize, London: Nominee Nominierung
2011 German Photo Book Award Deutscher Fotobuchpreis 2012: Gold
Photo Prize of the Alison and Peter Klein Foundation Stiftungspreis für Fotokunst der Alison und Peter Klein Stiftung: Finalist
2010 European Eyes on Japan by EU-Japan Fest: Awarded Grant Stipendium
2009 Prix Pictet, London: Nominee Nominierung
2007 Real Photography Award, Amsterdam: Nominee Nominierung
2005 Lead Awards, Hamburg: Gold
2004 Kunstpreis der Stadt Nordhorn, Nordhorn: Winner Preisträger
Phase One Prize, Vevey: Winner Gewinner
2003 Umbo Photo Prize, Lippstadt: Nominee Nominierung
KunstRai Prize, Amsterdam: Nominee Nominierung
European Architectural Photography Prize, Bonn: Honorable Mention Auszeichnung
2002 Peter Keetman Prize Peter-Keetman-Preis, Hamburg: Honorable Mention Auszeichnung
2001 Reinhart Wolf Award Reinhart-Wolf-Preis, Hamburg: Winner Preisträger

COLLECTIONS SAMMLUNGEN

Brandenburgische Kunstsammlungen, Cottbus
British American Tobacco Collection, London
Deutsche Bank Sammlung, Frankfurt am Main
DZ Bank Sammlung, Frankfurt am Main
Elgiz Collection, Istanbul
ev+a, Limerick, Ireland Irland
HSBC Trinkaus & Burkhardt AG, Berlin
Kunstmuseum Bonn, Bonn
Milwaukee Art Museum, Milwaukee, Wisconsin
Museum Franz Gertsch, Burgdorf, Switzerland Schweiz
National Gallery of Canada, Toronto
Nelson-Atkins Museum of Art, Kansas City, Missouri
Noorderlicht Photography Foundation, Groningen
Norton Museum, West Palm Beach, Florida
Saatchi Gallery, London
Sammlung Alison und Peter W. Klein, Nussdorf, Germany Deutschland
Sammlung Wemhöner, Herford
Städtische Galerie Nordhorn, Nordhorn
Taubman Museum of Art, Roanoke, Virginia
The New Art Gallery Walsall, Walsall, United Kingdom Großbritannien

DAVID CAMPANY

David Campany (*1967) is a writer and curator. His projects include the book and exhibition *a Handful of Dust* (2015), *The Open Road: Photography and the American Road Trip* (2014), *Walker Evans: The Magazine Work* (2014), *Jeff Wall: Picture for Women* (2011), *Photography and Cinema* (2008), and *Art and Photography* (2003). For his writing David has received the Alice Award, the ICP Infinity Award, the Krazsna-Krausz Award, and the Royal Photographic Society Award. He teaches at the University of Westminster, London.

David Campany (*1967) ist Autor und Kurator. Zu seinen Projekten gehören die Publikation und Ausstellung *A Handful of Dust* (2015), *The Open Road. Photography and the American Road Trip* (2014), *Walker Evans. The Magazine Work* (2014), *Jeff Wall. Picture for Women* (2011), *Photography and Cinema* (2008) und *Art and Photography* (2003). Für seine Tätigkeit als Schriftsteller hat Campany den Alice Award, den ICP Infinity Award, den Krazsna-Krausz Award sowie den Royal Photographic Society Award erhalten. Er lehrt an der University of Westminster, London.

ACKNOWLEDGMENTS DANK

A special thanks to Ellena Scheufler, to Sylvia Stulz-Rehbein, Thomas Rehbein, and Miriam Walgate from Thomas Rehbein Galerie, and to Nadine Barth, Cristina Steingräber, Julika Zimmermann, Nadine Schmidt, and the whole team from Hatje Cantz Verlag for their generous support of the book.
The artist would also like to thank Kristiana Balzer, Stephan Berg, Ben Burdett, David Campany, Jim Edwards, Gunter Gefeller, Corina Gertz, Jürgen Halfar, Markus Hartmann, Eva Haub, HSL, Bill Hunt, James Jeon, Dirk Lehr, Robin Merkisch, Roland Nachtigäller, the photographers from the *ISS,* Michael Reisch, Kris Scholz, Eva Steiniger, Gerd Stenmans, Andy de Sutter, Ingo Taubhorn, Mechthild Urmelt, Heiner Wemhöner, and Andreas Zimmermann.

Besonderer Dank an Ellena Scheufler, an Sylvia Stulz-Rehbein, Thomas Rehbein und Miriam Walgate von der Thomas Rehbein Galerie und an Nadine Barth, Cristina Steingräber, Julika Zimmermann, Nadine Schmidt und das ganze Team vom Hatje Cantz Verlag für ihre große Unterstützung des Buches.
Außerdem dankt der Künstler Kristiana Balzer, Stephan Berg, Ben Burdett, David Campany, Jim Edwards, den Fotografen der ISS, Gunter Gefeller, Corina Gertz, Jürgen Halfar, Markus Hartmann, Eva Haub, HSL, Bill Hunt, James Jeon, Dirk Lehr, Robin Merkisch, Roland Nachtigäller, Michael Reisch, Kris Scholz, Eva Steiniger, Gerd Stenmans, Andy de Sutter, Ingo Taubhorn, Mechthild Urmelt, Heiner Wemhöner und Andreas Zimmermann.

This catalogue is published on occasion of the exhibitions
Diese Publikation erscheint zu den Ausstellungen: *Andreas Gefeller*
Thomas Rehbein Galerie, Cologne Köln
April 15 – May 21, 2016 15. April – 21. Mai 2016
Momente der Auflösung – Fotografische Werke von Andreas Gefeller, Fabian Marti und Taiyo Onorato & Nico Krebs
Marta Herford, Herford
June 25 – October 9, 2016 25. Juni – 9. Oktober 2016

Copyediting Lektorat: Leina Gonzalez, Uta Barbara Ullrich
Translation Übersetzung: Alexandra Titze-Grabec
Graphic design and reproductions
Grafische Gestaltung und Reproduktionen: Andreas Gefeller
Typeface Schrift: Ciutadella
Production Herstellung: Nadine Schmidt, Hatje Cantz
Printing Druck: Offsetdruckerei Karl Grammlich GmbH, Pliezhausen
Paper Papier: Luxo Art Samt, 170 g/m²
Binding Buchbinderei: Lachenmaier GmbH, Reutlingen

Image courtesy of
Mit freundlicher Genehmigung von: Thomas Rehbein Galerie, Cologne Köln: all works alle Arbeiten
BP Gelsenkirchen GmbH: *IP 13, IP 15*
Image Science & Analysis Laboratory, NASA Johnson Space Center: *SV 01–SV 21*

Published by Erschienen im: Hatje Cantz Verlag
Zeppelinstrasse 32, 73760 Ostfildern, Germany Deutschland
T +49 711 4405-200 F +49 711 4405-220
www.hatjecantz.com
A Ganske Publishing Group company
Ein Unternehmen der Ganske Verlagsgruppe

Artist Edition Künstleredition: A limited, signed artist edition appears in the Gerd Hatje Edition, which is published in limited quantities. For more information, please contact us by telephone or at egh@hatjecantz.de.
In der Edition Gerd Hatje ist eine limitierte, signierte Künstleredition in Kleinauflage erschienen. Weiterführende Informationen sind unter der Kontaktadresse egh@hatjecantz.de oder telefonisch zu erfragen.

Hatje Cantz books are available internationally at selected bookstores. For more information about our distribution partners, please visit our website at www.hatjecantz.com.
ISBN 978-3-7757-4116-3
Printed in Germany

Cover illustration Umschlagabbildung: *FR 22*, 2014